D1367175

Cushion Plants for the Rock Garden

Duncan Lowe

B T Batsford Ltd, London

Acknowledgements

For their willing help with reference material, photographs and certain aspects of cultivation, I am indebted to:

Dr Hugh Barr, Brian Burrow, Alan Edwards, Brian Halliwell, Harry Jans, Michael Kammerlander, David Mowle, Dr John Richards, Robert Rolfe, Geoff Rollinson, Dr George Smith, Stan Taylor and Frank Tindall.

First published 1995

Typeset by David Seabourne
and printed in China

Published by
B.T. Batsford Ltd
4 Fitzhardinge Street
London WIH OAH

A catalogue record for this book is available from the British Library
ISBN 0 7134 7425 4

CONTENTS

Note: This book refers throughout to John Innes (J.I.) compost, a proprietary brand (UK). The author gives a recipe for an equivalent compost on page 106.

It is now more than thirty years since I began growing alpine and rock plants, and even in the early days I was already developing a special interest in the cushion types, or 'buns' as they are affectionately known. Later, when I travelled to see them, clinging like colourful barnacles to their native rocks, that special interest was intensified, and I am glad to say has never since faltered. Almost every year new and fascinating species are being brought back from far-off lands, as access to them steadily improves, with the result that in the cultivation of cushion plants there is never a lack of fresh material and stimulation.

Whilst all cushion plants form, more or less, a mound of closely-packed foliage, they have a wonderful diversity of size, leaf and flower, ranging from tiny, moss-like buttons spangled with miniature blooms, to pillow-sized hummocks bearing elegant floral sprays. Thanks to these differences in character a quite modest assortment of cushion species can provide flower from January to September and interest all the year round. Some would be worth growing even if they were never to produce a single bloom, just for the beauty of their form, and whether the desired growing place be a pot, window box, trough or garden bed, there are cushion plants suited to live there. For the gardener with very limited time (or skill) they include trouble-free, near-indestructible types, and at the other extreme, exquisite rarities which require all of the dedicated grower's determination and expertise to meet their needs.

This book begins with questions as to why and where cushion plants have evolved. These are answered with explanations based on our present understanding of natural events and processes, conscious of the complex sciences involved, but keeping these at a respectful distance. Having established an appreciation of the plants and their origins, there then follows an exploration of their character and behaviour, species by species, revealing what these hold for the grower. The ways and means of cultivation require careful, detailed explanation and have a chapter devoted to them. The same treatment is given to those things that can go wrong, through pests, diseases and other causes, with advice on the ways to recognize and combat them.

Whether the reader has only recently acquired an interest in cushions or is already smitten and eager to know and try more, I hope that what is offered in the pages to come will be both informative and helpful. The contents do not rely solely upon my own experience, but are also drawn from associations and friendships with other similarly involved, who have generously contributed from their knowledge and skills. The final selection of individual plants for inclusion, however, has been my own, and it is almost inevitable that personal leanings will have had their influence; consequently, for any exclusions which might be considered unjust or inappropriate I must take the blame.

CHAPTER 1

The where and why of cushion plants

Wherever fertile soil gives way to harsher earth or rock, it is likely that cushion plants will be found amongst any vegetation succeeding in living there. The cushion form is an adaptation enabling survival in conditions under which 'conventional' plants would perish, not necessarily due to any meagreness or water or food supplies, but from other hardships which might be imposed by wind, sun, ice or snow. Such habitats may exist from sea shore to mountain top and in desert to Arctic climates, and from all of them we have brought, to the garden, species that we wished to cultivate and enjoy. Very few were ignored by the original plant hunters

1. The author searching for cushion plants.

and it was left to the growers to discover and discard those which proved to be unsuitable or of no merit. In some cases the most reluctant to accept life in captivity were the most beautiful of their kind, so tantalizing that they could not be rejected. The needs of these most choice species are very special and there are still just a few continuing to defy cultivation, but much progress has been made and plants previously regarded as 'ungrowable' are now reasonably well established in our collections, though admittedly, for several, only due to the untiring care of enthusiasts.

Many cushion plants in cultivation are classed as 'Alpines', which is reasonable because the majority of them come to us

2. Typical hostile homeland of cushion plants.

from mountain regions. An understanding of why this form of plant is common in such terrain can be helpful in our attempts to grow them successfully. Battles for survival lie at the heart of the cushion's evolution, as they do for many highly specialized life forms, and the following is an attempt to reconstruct those battles and the happenings which caused the cushions to be where they now are and why they have remained there.

Most cushions belong to families containing 'normally formed' plants; for instance, there is a crassula which grows as a dense, low hump and is quite hardy in our British winters without any assistance, yet other cultivated species of the same genus are inmates of the greenhouse and can reach a metre in height. Similarly, there are rock-dwelling saxifrages which make immaculate cushions, but have large-leaved, tall-stemmed cousins living in woodland and in marshy ground. These contrasts tell us that some species have had to alter dramatically in character and behaviour in order to survive, and fossil records indicate that the changes were from long-stemmed structures to compact hummocks rather than reverse.

Tall stalks and large leaves are vulnerable to strong winds, as they are also to dehydration, sliding snow, shuttering stones and combinations of these. Lower growth and tighter, smaller foliage are less prone to damage from such forces and so a trend to evolve in a dwarfing, huddled manner is in the right direction. To say that the cushion is thus the ultimate form achievable would, however, be misleading, as another shape which serves just as well under the attacks described is the creeping mat, adopted by such plants as *Saxifraga oppositifolia* and *Linaria alpina*.

AGAINST THE ICE

Ice ages are catastrophic events, obliterating whole races of living things for ever, and when the vast sheets of frozen water eventually retreat, they leave behind tracts of spoil and bare rock that are, initially, almost devoid of life. But, waiting for thousands of years at the limit of the ice, where the ground is still fairly hostile but just habitable, are the survivors, who during that long sojourn have been developing their capabilities to endure, and with the coming of the great thaw are ready to advance. These early colonizers must be tough and able to subsist on the barest of essentials. The first to pioneer the new land will be the lichens and mosses, but the cushion plants are unlikely to be far behind. To appreciate why they would be amongst the early settlers we need to look carefully at a typical cushion plant.

CHARACTER FOR SURVIVAL

Take first of all the shape itself, which is basically a dome, approximating to a half sphere. Compared to a cube, a pyramid, a cylinder or similar shapes the half sphere is superior to them all in that it uses the least amount of material to contain the same volume. In this form the plant exposes the minimum possible surface area to whatever the climate or environment may produce, and in addition presents a smooth, curved, low-resistance profile; what better defence against the hazards of nature? In the rough and tumble of real life on the rocks cushions are sometimes obliged to deviate from the ideal shape due to some obstacle or fault in the spot where they are growing, but given a reasonably even, open surface for an anchorage, the plant will try very hard to create a near-perfect dome. Occasionally several closely-neighbouring plants of the same species may join up to form a humpy tuffet; however, with further growth there comes a communal effort to fill in the joints and eventually achieve, as near as possible, a smooth single mound. Such is the inherent reaction of the plants to equip themselves with the very best protection.

The growth of a cushion is a slow process, particularly in the early stages. It begins, typically, with the formation of a single rosette or tuft of leaves, which is often all that is attained in the first year (Fig. 1a). In the second year the stem lengthens a little as the growing tip produces new leaves and adds one or two side shoots, and whilst this is happening the previous year's leaves wither, but (most importantly) stay in place (Fig. 1b). The same pattern is followed in the third year, the side shoots becoming branches of the original stem (Fig. 1c) and a juvenile cushion becomes recognizable. Successive growth occurs in the same manner as each season passes, slowly increasing the plant's size, until drought, disease, rockfall or simple old age brings the process to an end. Not surprisingly virtually all cushion plants are perennial and essentially evergreen.

The adult life can be surprisingly long, an extreme example being provided by a silver-leaved, hummock-making raoulia native to the mountains of New Zealand. Reputed to live for centuries, this species can reach large proportions and is known by the New Zealanders as the 'Vegetable Sheep', which gives a measure of its size.

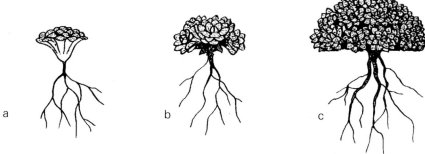

Fig. 1 **The progression of a seedling: (a) first year; (b) second year; (c) third year.**

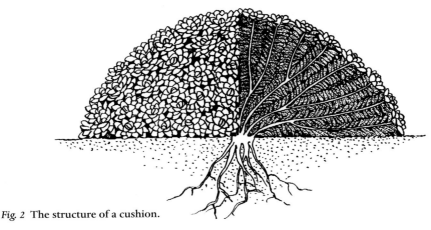

Fig. 2 **The structure of a cushion.**

SELF-PROTECTION

Regardless of how big or how small they are, all cushions are composed mainly of dead material. Above ground level the only living elements are the thin stems radiating out from the root-stock and the terminal rosettes or tufts of leaves at the ends of those stems, the remainder consisting entirely of the lifeless, but retained foliage of previous years, combining to form a spongy core (Fig. 2). Not surprisingly, the benefit to the cushion in having such a fibrous, dense interior is resilience, often crucial to existence if the plant lives on an unstable cliff or scree (as is often the case), where stones frequently rattle down and bombard the residents. The strength of the core structure, combined with its resilience and aided by the domed shape, serves the plant well when the weight of a considerable depth of snow bears upon it, and that is quite a common burden for mountain-dwelling species in winter.

A HOLD ON LIFE

In its underground parts the cushion plant is equally well specialized for survival in tough conditions. For the great majority of plant types it is usual for the amount of living material below ground to be roughly the same as that above it, both in quantity and spread. Many cushion-forming species do not have such similar proportions and can generate a root system up to four times greater in extent than the growth above ground. There are two quite distinct rooting types, equally effective but suited to different opportunities offered by frugal habitats; they can be called the 'delving' type and the 'searching' type. The first of these employs either a single stout tap root or a few tough, fleshy thongs, to drive deeply into rock crevices or beds of fragmented stone. For the most part these roots are penetrating tools, designed to deploy the water and food-gathering parts to sources well below the surface and also to effect a firm anchorage that will hold good for the lifetime of the plant. The alternative is a widely-spread network of hair-fine roots capable of exploring the thinnest of fissures and reaching equally as far as the 'delving' forms. In both types the system has to be extensive and highly efficient if it is to discover and extract sustenance, for there is often little or no soil as such, and only a thinly-spread deposit of nutrients to be had. Where the habitat is in a region of low rainfall, the same far-reaching systems are utilized to seek out and take up deeply-held reserves of moisture.

Because the tap or thong root can also

act as a storage organ, the plants adopting this form are better able to survive in coarse rubble and in more arid conditions than the fine-rooted 'searchers', but the latter can infiltrate the narrowest of fractures, denied to the 'delvers', and so are most often found on hard shales and other finely-faulted rocks. On soft shales and gravels neither type seems to have an advantage, both appearing to fare equally well in such places. As anchoring devices there is little to choose between the two systems, for whilst the 'delver' has great strength in a single root strand, the 'searcher' achieves the same end on the principle of strength in numbers.

The final survival feature is the means by which the cushion plant reproduces to ensure continuity and this involves, in most cases, its crowning glory: the flower.

3. Only the eternal snows halt the pioneering cushions.

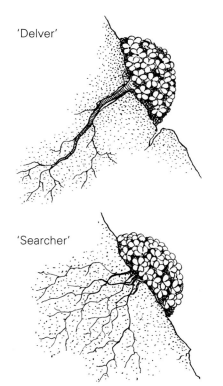

Fig. 3 **The two basic rooting systems of cushion plants.**

THE URGE TO SURVIVE

There is no shortage of insects even in the most hostile of environments, whether on a bleak mountainside or a desert outcrop, so the use of flowers as the instruments of reproduction is almost universal amongst the cushions; the hazard is to the seed produced by the process. On the type of terrain already discussed the likelihood of a seed lodging in a spot favourable to germination is slim, and for subsequent growth even slimmer. In response to such unfavourable prospects it is common for the plants to produce large quantities of seed in proportion to their size, to which end they must flower abundantly, thereby creating one of their greatest attractions for us, the growers. At the time of blooming the cushion can, in some species, be entirely covered in flowers, with not a leaf visible. The sight of a healthy plant growing out of a knife-thin crack in a huge and otherwise solid granite slab sets one to wonder just how the original seed got there and, even more mystifying, how it found enough sustenance to develop and prosper, year after year. Some believe that the wind-scattered or rain-washed seed might be ensnared by a spider's web, at least to fix it in the crevice, but as to how it then managed to avoid death whilst it sent out its tiny root and raised seed leaves, still wants for a credible explanation.

In high altitudes and high latitudes, where the spring comes late and the winter early, the growing season can be as short as three months, during which growth, flowering and seed setting must all be accomplished. This is less than half the time available to plants in easier environments. In consequence the flowers are often developed before any other part of the plant begins to grow, thus ensuring that the time available for seed production is as long as possible. After this brief and hectic activity, however, a long rest is in store and the cushion enters a dormant state with its life systems barely functioning. During the long sleep the plant may be buried under a deep layer of protective snow, safe from icy gales, pests and other foes, waiting in the dark for the far-off spring. On the other hand, if the habitat is on a mountain ridge or similarly exposed site where snow cannot lie, the plant must endure the worst of an Alpine or perhaps Arctic winter. The hardiness of any species capable of living through such conditions is unquestioned, but it should also be remembered that in those wild winters it is too cold for rain to fall or for water to lie, hence the cushion is never saturated during dormancy, a fact that is of great importance to the way it is treated in cultivation. In the brief summer the same plant may have to withstand intense, dehydrating sunlight for many days during a dry period; the clear thin air

of the altitudes is much less of a filter and shield than our lowland atmosphere. It is believed by some that the hairiness common to quite a number of cushion species may be as much a protection against strong sun as it is against intense cold or drying winds, but opponents point out that not all the plants accustomed to strong sunshine are hairy – and the debate continues!

THE ESSENTIAL CUSHION

We now return to the receding ice and the wilderness it leaves behind, which will be slowly populated by plant life. Eventually the harsh landscape will be softened as soils build up and grasses, herbs, shrubs and trees find acceptable conditions. The highly adapted, specialized cushions and other plants of spartan conditions are not equipped to compete with new, strong, advancing rivals and must retreat with the glaciers to the mountains, or hold out wherever the rock still stands clear of the vegetation, where their abilities and protective features remain advantageous. They hold their ground on sea cliffs, the walls of gorges and rocky banks, wherever their competitors are unable to follow. All such havens have sustained the cushion plants, which is why we find them there today.

Although still fairly frugal in nature, some of the lower refuges are more congenial, being either less windswept, or scorched, or frozen and their cushion plant residents have responded accordingly. In sheltered niches foliage can be softer and the flowers may rise on slender stems. Amongst the rocks of Alpine foothills, where the summers are longer and drier, leaves are often leathery or spiky and sometimes coated in various ways to conserve moisture, but the blooms may be quite extravagant, in long, arching sprays or cascades, adorning the cliffs and boulders, safe from the gales of the heights.

There are interesting and at times puzzling patterns of distribution, where certain species behave unexpectedly. Some occur at fairly modest elevations but also climb to high mountain habitats. Others have a similar range, being found at lower and higher levels, but not in between. In both cases there can be differences in character and hardiness in the high- and low-dwelling types. Similar gaps occur horizontally, where a species may inhabit two or more locations in very similar habitats, but which are separated by considerable distances. Ice movements are thought to be mainly responsible for these estrangements and where the isolation of each colony has lasted for many thousands of years, independent evolution brings changes which are unique to each location. In the European mountains the 'gap' between communities can be as much as a hundred or so kilometres, but in extreme instances the same species is native to different continents!

- Having now completed this brief study of form, habit and behaviour, we can portray, in a few sentences, the essential cushion:
- It has evolved from taller, larger-leaved ancestors to become a squat, spartan form suited for survival in severe habitats.
- Its common shape is a dome, varying in size and firmness from species to species.

- It is evergreen and relatively long-lived.
- It often flowers and seeds profusely.
- It is, in most cases, completely hardy, but may be unaccustomed to wetness whilst inactive.

DECISIONS

In deciding which plants should and should not be included for description and discussion under this book's title, it became clear that some sort of definition for a cushion plant was desirable, otherwise there would be a danger of following the simple logic that argues: 'all cushion plants are domes, therefore all domes are cushion plants'. This is quite often the case in gardening and botanical literature, but if it were to be applied here it would promote the inclusion of plants and shrubs which are outside the intended subjects and aims.

The term 'dome-shaped', which has been very convenient so far, is rather too precise for a workable definition, as it is not unusual to find impeccably qualified cushions becoming elongated or multi-humped under certain circumstances. Crevice-dwelling types can sometimes elongate when growth follows the crack in which the plant is living, producing a profile something like a halved pear, or perhaps several plants may join to form a humpy ribbon along a rock fissure. Nevertheless there will be some instances where the words 'domed' or 'dome' will be appropriate to describe a shape and therefore they will not be discarded.

In the previous chapter the explanation of cushion plant characteristics have, in fact, produced the ingredients for an adequate definition and with a little refinement they will serve well enough. Hopefully then, it is sufficient to say that from here on a cushion plant is one which:

(a) tends to form a hemispherical mound, but can be distorted by external influences,

(b) has a dense core of dead (but retained) leaves held on living stems rising from a central root-stock,

(c) has a relatively even surface, comprised of closely-packed rosettes or tufts of living foliage.

Inevitably, having arrived at the qualifying features, the borderline types and variants which do not quite measure up to the definition are immediately apparent and it becomes necessary to offer some justification for their inclusion. Here, then, are the arguments:

■ Quite a few cushion plants can, under certain circumstances, take on a more mat-like form, but unless the cushion version is in the minority, these 'alternating' types are accepted.

■ One or two very dwarf shrubs, whose centres are composed mainly of congested, twiggy growth, have also escaped rejection because in all other respects they conform and are also greatly valued by many enthusiastic growers.

■ There are hard cushions which can be fondly patted without coming to any harm at all, but others, of a softer, spongy make-up, may suffer injury from the smallest of inquisitive fingers. Nevertheless, both types have a 'dense' cores, in the sense of being crowded, thus meeting the qualifying requirement.

■ Some species have a central root-stock when young, but later may root down from their basal stems where there is opportunity to do so. Such behaviour is quite common in several groups of true cushion plants.

Before finalizing the selection of plants for inclusion, two aspects of a practical nature had also to be taken into account. These were their merit and their availability, for there seemed little to be gained in lengthening the text to include species which might be botanically interesting, but otherwise had little to recommend them. Nor did there appear to be much point in describing rarities which, other than in their natural occurrence, exist exclusively as cherished specimens in the collections of a few experts and are unlikely ever to become obtainable. With such plants excluded the reader is presented with just those which are both worth growing and reasonably available. Acquiring some of the rarer species will probably involve searches of nursery stocks or obtaining and raising seed, but these can be enjoyable pursuits.

The final decision concerned the manner of presentation. Where a genus contains a significant number of cushion-forming species it seemed logical to present them as a group (eg androsaces, drabas, saxifrages). Of course, their discussion will identify each of the plants making up the group to give the reader a portrait of each individual, noting its particular needs, merits, fads and so on. The remaining plants can then be addressed singly; these will be either the odd cushion-forming species from genera which are otherwise 'conventional' in form, or genera represented by very small numbers for other reasons. Thus we have 'Groups' and what we can call 'Oddfellows' as headings for the chapters into which the divisions fall.

CHAPTER 2

The cushion plant 'groups'

THE ANDROSACES

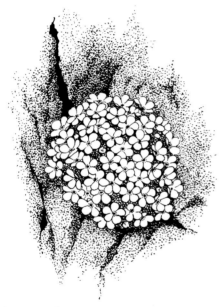

A race of true mountain plants, the androsaces have perfected the ability to live in the most awesome places, from the boulder fields and stone slopes to the crags and summit ridges of the high peaks. Some only cease their climbing quest for habitable perches when they meet the edge of the eternal snows, and even then will occasionally colonize rocks which, in an unusually cool summer, may remain snow-covered. There are accounts of these over-ambitious individuals actually surviving a missed growing season, going dormant under the autumn snows of one year, staying covered for the whole of the next year and emerging unscathed in July of the year following; a hibernation period of some twenty-one months! Whether or not they could tolerate an ever longer period of privation is uncertain. In the European Alps the altitude limit for androsaces is around 4000 m (13000 ft) but in the Himalayas they have been discovered at heights in excess of 5500 m (18000 ft). All the species living at great elevations are cushion-forming, and often the higher they live the more compact their growth and the more profuse their flowering. A feature of these high-dwelling forms is the lack of any visible flower stem, and the open petals sit tightly on the cushion surfaces, sometimes crowding and overlapping to create a solid blanket of bloom over the entire plant. The sight of such abundance and beauty in a stark rock crevice is unforgettable.

Not surprisingly, in our garden environments the special survival functions of high mountain androsaces become confused. The period over which temperatures are conducive to growth is longer than that to which the plants are accustomed; in fact more than twice as long, and this imposes a strain by extending the active state, with telling consequences. Instead of a single concentrated burst of spring flowering, there may be additional attempts later in the season, or the whole process may become stretched over a long period, both of which put great demands on the resources of the plant. Another reaction can be the development of much

4. *Androsace alpina*, in its high altitude form.
5. The less huddled profile of plants at lower levels.

more growth, further draining the available energy. When the plant is finally able to rest, as temperatures fall and days grow shorter, it may do so in a weaker state than is safe for its health. There is little we can do about our climate, short of moving home and garden to an Alpine retreat, but by protecting the androsaces from pests and diseases as far as is practicable, and shielding them from damaging weather effects where this is feasible, we help them to survive.

Beset by foes and conditions never encountered in their native habitats, it seems little short of a miracle that the androsaces can not only be maintained in cultivation, but also coaxed into flowering almost as perfectly as they do in the wild. Small wonder that they are regarded by many as the 'aristocrats' of the cushions. The basics of successful cultivation and the manner in which we can give all possible help will be revealed as each species is presented and described, and we begin with one of the finest of the race.

Androsace alpina

In places this species descends the mountains far enough to be reached by road, but its best forms live in the gravels and shales of stony wastes at greater altitudes. Along almost the entire length of the European Alps *A. alpina* has found acceptable habitats and although recorded in a few calcareous locations, it is primarily an inhabitant of granites and other acid rock formations. This preference is nowhere more apparent than on the great volcanic ridge of the Bindelweg in the Dolomites, where it thrives in the black rubble of eroding lava, yet is absent from the surrounding limestone crags. At the lower levels its growth is inclined to be mat-like, but with increase in height comes a compaction of form, producing low-domed to almost hemispherical cushions.

The slightly fleshy foliage is a fresh pea-green, but describing the colour of the flowers is not so easy, for they range from a rich rose, through delicate pinks, to pure white, all complemented by a clear yellow eye. What is more, several of these hues can be displayed by a single plant, due to the gentle fading that comes with the ageing of the flower. This delightful diversity adds to the pleasure of raising plants from seed, which is by far the surest means of acquiring healthy infants; cuttings taken from an adult never seem to have the same vigour or life expectancy.

It was mentioned earlier that some of the cushion types have the habit of rooting down from ground-level shoots and *A. alpina* is one of those likely to do so; a fact worth remembering when preparing a growing place for this plant, whether in a bed, trough or pot. Any attempt to simulate the natural rooting substance, which consists of little but grit and fragmented stone, fails miserably and as yet the best results are achieved with a mixture of sandy loam, leafmould and coarse grit, in equal volumes. Alternatively John Innes (J.I.) No. 1 (see page 106), blended with an equal bulk of non-limy grit, will often suffice. *A. alpina* craves for light, needing as much sunshine as it is possible to provide; a cover of glass will reduce the quality of light enough to cause lax growth, lack of bloom and loss of vigour. Some growers, whilst agreeing with the latter, believe that a glass cover is beneficial in the winter months and this may well be so in other regions and climates, but as yet, personal experience confirms that the best results are achieved

in unprotected troughs. Even in a fully open position, in a good summer, the leaf rosettes will never cluster as tightly as they should, nor will crowded flowers hide the cushion, but though its growth could be tighter and its blooms more numerous it is still beautiful and well worth growing. Put it in a sunny trough, defend it against aphids, accept that it will be short-lived and *A. alpina* will do its best to please, contributing self-sown seedlings for your added enjoyment.

Androsace brevis

Included because it is a cushion-former, albeit rather flat and loose, but its treatment will be brief, for reasons that will become evident. Related to *A. alpina* and resembling it to some extent, this is a relatively rare species, existing only as a few colonies on mountains near Lake Como in Italy. It is notoriously difficult in cultivation, with an aversion to pots and glass cover. In the wild its life-span is short and in captivity even shorter. So far it has responded best to life in a scree bed or trough with no form of winter protection, enduring almost three years, growing big enough to cover two thumbnails and producing five cherry-pink flowers. A definite challenge for the enthusiast.

Androsace carnea

Such is the variation of this species that the botanists have divided it into four subspecies. All make cushions (with differing degrees of success) and flower in small umbels held on stems above the foliage, but the best of them is *A. carnea* ssp. *laggeri*. Its home is in the high valleys of the Pyrenees, where, as soon as the sun has cleared away the snow cover, the short turf is freckled with the intense pink of this small plant. The tufts of dark green leaves are tightly bunched to create a firm, well-shaped cushion which, in old age, may reach as much as 10 cm (4 in) across.

6. Native only to the Pyrenees – *Androsace ciliata.*

As a garden plant it has good qualities, being quite hardy and wanting only a reasonably sunny spot in lime-free, gritty soil; it needs no protection whatsoever from the elements. Where garden conditions are to its liking the androsace can live for several years, slowly building up a solid mound and flowering promptly every April; and because the blooms open in a succession rather than a single burst, they give colour for three or four weeks. They are also pleasingly weather-resistant. There are no reasons why it should not be grown in a pot, but as it is so responsive and needs so little attention, there seems little point in doing so unless it be for exhibition.

The other three members of the group are: *A. carnea* ssp. *rosea*, from the Massif Central, *A. carnea* ssp. *carnea* from the Alps and *A. carnea* ssp. *brigantiaca*, again from the Alps, but white-flowered whereas the other two are pink. All three carry their flowers much as *A. carnea* ssp. *laggeri*, but *brigantiaca* is too long in the stem for real charm.

Androsace ciliata

Go in summer to the central mountains of the Pyrenees and climb very high, until the last of the turf has been left behind and all around is a wilderness of rock with snow still lying in the gullies; only then is it worth hunting. Look for a startling splash of bright rose amongst the shattered stone; go closer to see the immaculate cluster of flowers almost hiding a mound of closely-knit foliage. You have found *Androsace ciliata*. By the standards of the genus this species is fairly quick-growing when brought into cultivation and it is not difficult to raise from seed or to root single rosettes in a propagator, but of all the race it is foremost in attracting and suffering from aphids. So pronounced is this vulnerability that it can be utilized as an 'early warning device' in a collection of alpines: the grower only needs to check *A. ciliata* and if it clear then the chances are high that all is well generally. If, on the other hand, the pest is found, action can be taken to repel the attack before it can take hold.

Aside from keeping sap-suckers at bay, the cultivation is fairly straightforward to begin with. Half-and-half soil mixtures (50% organic and 50% drainage material) produce good results, whether in a container or an alpine bed, and in direct light the plant will usually flower generously. The older and larger it becomes, however, the more skill and attention is needed to maintain its well-being. In addition to requiring potting-on at least once per year, an adult specimen will want extra sustenance, most easily supplied through a liquid feed every three or four weeks in the growing season. A low-nitrogen fertilizer, such as those developed for tomatoes or roses, applied at half recommended strength, is as good as anything. The plant can be grown equally well in a raised bed or trough, asking only for winter cover and, of course, the attention of the aphid patrol. Pot-grown plants need the same protection whilst in a state of low-ebb, from late October to March. In all cases any rosettes which are wilting, yellowing or showing signs of mould should be promptly removed.

The natural variation in flower colour, quality and quantity is quite marked; even in a small batch of seedlings there are often good, bad and indifferent forms. Also variable is their constitution, where it will be found that some have better resistance to the alien climate of the garden than others. The best solution to these vagaries is to grow a number of plants in a number of differing situations (they do not take up much space) and propagate from the pick of the survivors. Do not expect *A. ciliata* to live much longer than four or five years in cultivation and be pleased if it does so.

Androsace cylindrica

Monsieur De Candolle, who was responsible for naming this delightful species, must have been unfortunate in having specimens which had struggled to exist in a far from ideal location. Under adverse circumstances the plants are unable to build up a solid cushion and grow instead as a few stumpy stems, which, year by year, fail to branch and just elongate a little, holding on to their old, dried leaves, forming – yes – cylinders (see Fig. 4). This stunted habit is not normal, confirmed by more recent field studies in which it has been seen that better-placed examples make rounded humps of their narrow-leaved rosettes.

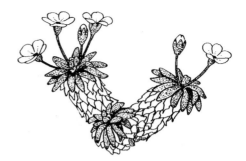

Fig. 4 *Androsace cylindrica* in an extreme form.

The habitats are few and scattered along the sub-Alpine levels of the Pyrenees, from the central regions westwards, one or two being so low as to lie within the wooded areas. All locations are on calcareous rocks. So small and localized are the surviving colonies that the species is regarded by many as endangered. Over-zealous collecting could be the main cause of the scarcity, for although *A. cylindrica* may not be the most prized, it is certainly amongst those sought by the keen growers. Its charm is easily appreciated when seen in full bloom, with as many as ten flowers rising from each rosette on short stems. The result is a canopy of blossom, which trembles attractively to every movement of the air.

This is not a plant for the open garden, but can be grown satisfactorily in a specially-prepared bed with winter cover. Generally, however, it is grown as a pot subject, either in an alpine house or a plunge frame, using mixtures of simple make-up for the rooting medium, such as equal parts of J.I. No. 2 (see page 106) and coarse grit. Unlike so many cushion species it does not appreciate full exposure to the sun and should be lightly shaded during the hottest hours of the day. Seed is usually set in large amounts and should germinate readily. There are well-qualified reports of a pink-flowered form with supporting photographs, yet it has eluded all recent efforts to find it; some suspect that the plant seen was a hybrid of *A. cylindrica* and *A. ciliata*.

Androsace delavayi

Away now to the Himalayas for an androsace which fills the air around it with the scent of almonds. It is an inhabitant of the high screes and moraines up to 5500 m (18000 ft) and also rock crevices at similar altitudes. The leaf-rosettes look like tiny lettuce hearts and crowd tightly together to form a smooth dome, upon which sit the stemless white flowers in profusion.

When this species was first brought into cultivation by early expeditions into Nepal, the rate of growth was surprisingly rapid. By its third spring it had developed from a rooted fragment into a cushion 15 cm (6 in) across and was characteristically covered in flower. Increase was made easy by the willingness of the single rosettes to root when used as cuttings, but then came a decline in vigour, both of the offspring and the parent, coupled with a fall-off in flower. No clear cause for the deterioration was identified, although it was suspected that our lowland viruses might be involved, particularly as even those plants raised from the occasionally set seed were also afflicted. Thankfully the effect was not terminal, though the stock was weakened and less easy to maintain. Fresh introductions of seed from the wild have come to us recently, bringing with them new hopes and more material to work on. As yet, with only a partial success as experience, it is difficult to make recommendations regarding culture; what can be noted is that: (a) without full light the plant becomes lax, drawn and reluctant to flower, (b) whilst dormant it must never be allowed to approach dryness at the root, (c) aphid attack can progress unseen and is exceptionally weakening to the plant at all times of the year. Other factors

such as soil mixtures, watering, feeding and shelter are still in the trial and error stages.

Androsace globifera

Another Himalayan, but one which shuns the bare rocks and is accustomed to grassy slopes between the 3500 m and 4500 m contour lines (11000–15000 ft) where it is regularly saturated every afternoon by the monsoon rains. In these high meadows *A. globifera* makes tight cushions which can become of considerable size, as low mounds some one or more metres across. Their flowering is uninhibited and because the colonies are extensive, whole hillsides can be mottled with lilac pink during the blooming period.

Cultivated plants hint at their ambition for size by their quite strong growth and regular demands for more rooting space. Pot culture tends to be restrictive, unless moving on to increasingly larger pots is carried out with unusual frequency; the happiest specimens seem to be those given a place in a raised bed where they can root as they wish. Most cultivated plants quickly achieve an eye-catching hemispherical form that is a thing of beauty in itself, being smooth, compact and a pleasing fir-green in colour. No amount of rain appears to be too much for them in the season of growth, which is hardly surprising when remembering their monsoon-watered homeland, but a protecting cover of glass is necessary from early autumn to early spring if they are not to suffer the attentions of moulds that thrive on soggy foliage. Our British summers somehow lack whatever it is that bring about the all-over flowering that is typical of the wild plant and it is likely that strength of sunlight is to blame. Even though the Himalayan summer brings its daily dousing to the home ground of *A. globifera*, the mornings are fine and the strong sunlight beats down through clear, thin air. Unless there is some treatment still to be discovered which will give the plants that mystical boost, we must be content with a spangling of bloom and enjoy it.

To provide a substitute for the earth of the mountain flank, soil mixtures need to be very well drained yet amply provided with humus and nutrients, to satisfy the appetites of this androsace. One which has proved effective is a blend of J.I. No. 2 (or light loam), leafmould (or peat, etc.) and coarse grit, in equal proportions. None of the ingredients should be limy. The latter is offered with pot culture in mind; in raised beds the mixture is not so precise and provided that the 'soil' content is about the same as that of the gravel or fine chippings used, the plant will seek out what it needs with its unrestricted roots.

Androsace hausmannii

Nobody will ever grow this androsace for the sheer symmetry of its cushion or its floral abundance. It is the 'Tiny Tim' of the family, with a charming habit of setting its white flowers in a garland around the small, globular hump of its grey-green leaves. The Dolomites are its home, where it anchors in limestone crevices and screes, at times maturing into an almost spherical shape. The life expectancy of the wild plant is thought to be only four or five years and in cultivation is likely to be less, but it is worth a place, especially where it is not in competition with other, larger species. Plant it then in a crevice, contrived from well-placed stones or perhaps in a block of tufa, and do not shade it overmuch from the sun. Though its stay may be short, it will almost certainly provide you with some excellent seed to compensate for its passing.

Androsace hedraeantha

From the high turf and summit stones of mountains in the central Balkans comes this small tuffet with features very much like A. carnea ssp. rosea, which has already been introduced. The flowers are usually pink with a hint of violet, but can occasionally be white. It is rarely seen in cultivation yet is no more difficult to please than the A. carnea types and responds to the same treatment.

Androsace helvetica

As the name implies, Switzerland has claimed this superb species for its own, which is understandable to anyone who has seen the plant in its hundreds and at its very best, on the summit ridges of the Bernese Oberland. There, on flaking and fractured rock, it grows slowly and endures long, wedged in fissures and crannies well lit by the sun. The cushions are wonderfully tight and solid and whilst some spend their long dormancy under a shielding snow mantle, others are fully exposed to the year-round weathers, yet this seems to cause no differences in behaviour between them. With the coming of spring to the heights, which typically is in mid- to late July, the cushions rush into bloom with a covering of milky-white, golden-eyed flowers held hard against the foliage. Only when these have been pollinated and the seed-making process is under way do the plants turn to adding a little new growth in the short time left to them before winter returns.

Success in persuading A. helvetica to grow and flower in our ridiculously contrasting climate and conditions owes much, initially, to selection.

A crop of seed-raised plants will generally show individual traits, especially if the seed comes from gatherings made in the wild. Some will soon reveal a tendency to fall prey to disease, others will be reluctant to flower and there will be frustrating combinations, such as promising flow-erers prone to ills and decay-resistant forms unwilling to bloom. With luck there may be one or two possessing the two virtues of floriferousness and resis-tance to disease, and these are the ones to retain and cherish. We have been growing this androsace a long time and there is little doubt that for the best results it should be kept at all times under glass. The alpine house is the obvious haven but a well ventilated plunge bed, roofed with glass, serves just as well and in some cases better. Any expansion on this manner of growing, made here, would only pre-empt the content of a later chapter; suffi-cient then to say that for *A. helvetica* the potting compost should be nour-ishing, but very well drained. Skilled growers have nurtured prize specimens to venerable size and age; one in particular was a constant feature of the show benches and at its zenith was a smooth mound almost a hand's-span in diameter, covered in flowers to celebrate its eleventh birthday!

Androsace hirtella

Loosely translated *hirtella* means 'min-utely hairy' or 'somewhat shaggy'. Why this particular species should be thus iden-tified is unclear, considering that all the other cushion androsaces are also hairy to a greater or lesser extent. A more promi-nent and pleasing feature of *A. hirtella* is the almond scent of its flowers, and how intriguing that this same perfume should be produced by another species (*A. delavayi*), which is not closely related and lives far away in Nepal. The haunts of *A. hirtella* are small and few, scattered along the Pyrenean chain and always on limestone cliffs. Its flowers are a cool white and stand slightly above the firm cushion on short stems.

Whilst this lovely and elegant andro-sace is justly regarded as being amongst the most choice, it is somewhat easier to maintain than most of the elite and it therefore seems strange that it should be seldom seen in cultivation. The cause of this rarity may lie in its promiscuous behaviour with another Pyrenean species, for if *A. cylindrica* is in the vicinity at flow-ering time, it can be almost guaranteed that cross-pollination will occur and any offspring raised from the seed will be suspect. Many plants grown and labelled as *A. hirtella* are close to, but not quite, the real thing, though every bit as pleasing in character and appearance.

Androsace muscoidea

A species with such variation that it can grow as a carpeting mat or an immaculate hemispherical cushion. Until the introduc-tions of recent years brought us a wealth of types to grow and study, the only form of *A. muscoidea* available was a white-flow-ered clone which grew as a shallow mound of stoloniferous rosettes. The newcomers added pinks and carmines to the colour range and habits from sprawling mats to tight humps, together with stemless to long-stalked flowers. Alas, many were prone to diseases or the British climate and could not be sustained. Only a very few have become truly estab-lished in cultivation, but, happily, two of these survivors are fine cushion makers. The first of these is so downy with leaf hairs that it takes on a silvery sheen in the growing season and is studded with stem-less white flowers of good substance. It has no official sub-species rank, but is known as the 'Schacht form', in recogni-tion of its discoverer Dieter Schacht, who brought it back from the mountains of Kashmir. Such has been its response to cultivation that it is now offered by the specialist nursery trade. The second sur-vivor is a distinct form of the species, namely *A. muscoidea* forma *longiscapa*, which has a lovely colour range from lilac to a deep cherry-red, and in the best clones grows as a compact mound. It blooms in small open umbels on wiry stalks and can be very floriferous.

The 'Schacht form' is trouble-free in its youth, needing only a cover against winter wet, but as it matures, is really a subject for the alpine house or roofed plunge bed. Its homeland lies at the drier end of the Himalayas where this plant frequents stony slopes and gravelly meadows. In contrast the *longiscapa* form hails from the monsoon-affected flanks further east, in Nepal, and revels in summer rain at all stages of its development. It abhors alpine house conditions when in growth and even in winter prefers an airy plunge frame, or better still a raised bed with a rain cover. Both forms fare well in half-and-half mixtures of fibrous soil and grit, provided that the lime content is low.

Androsace pubescens

Of all the European androsaces, few can be as seldom seen, even in specialist collections, as this member of the family, not because it is particularly rare in nature but, it would seem, due its dislike of cultivation. Why it has this resentment is hard to understand, when it can be found sharing the same habitat with *A. helvetica* and *A. alpina* in several regions of the western Alps. Many is the proud owner who has brought to the alpine plant shows what proves to be an imposter bearing the *A. pubescens* label, yet it is not very difficult to identify. The true plant has leaf-rosettes which are more open and less tightly-packed than those of *A. helvetica* or the hybrids of *A. hirtella* × *A. cylindrica*, with which it is so often confused. The shape and array of the leaf rosettes bear a resemblance to those of a sempervivum. A much smaller detail for recognition is the presence of forked hairs on the leaf surface.

In the wild the plants usually bloom well and can cover the greyish-green cushion with a cap of their pure-white flowers, which have a greenish-yellow eye and notched, blunt petals. Despite what the name (*pubescens*) suggests, only some specimens are covered with hair to the extent of being downy; on others the effect can be less hirsute.

When the most skilled of growers repeatedly fail to keep this species, what can be offered in the way of cultural advice? Logically the care and treatment given to, say, *A. helvetica*, should be at least a sound basis for further work in coaxing such a comely but reluctant androsace to stay with us.

Androsace pyrenaica

An aptly-named and charming species which lives in the Pyrenees and nowhere else, but it is by no means widespread in those mountains. Search for it around the central peaks, from 2500 m (8000 ft) to the high crests, ignoring areas where the rock is calcareous. Sheltered fissures and crannies in granite cliffs offer the only acceptable homes to this elusive plant and even there *A. pyrenaica* occurs only in small, scattered colonies which can be difficult to find and dangerous to reach. Out of flower the plants are very easily overlooked, the dark-green cushions hard to discern against the stained and lichen-mottled stone. When in bloom, however, their hideouts are betrayed as light catches the little buns of starry flowers lodged in the sombre rocks.

The scarcity and very exacting needs of the wild plants might well be viewed as a forewarning of difficulties in cultivation, yet they are no more taxing to grow and flower than their near relations. In its early years *A. pyrenaica* will respond well to the treatment already described for *A. cylindrica* and shares that species' appreciation of midday shade. After three or

7. A venerable specimen of *Androsace pyrenaica*.

four years mature specimens require more care and attention to maintain their well-being (see Chapter 4). This androsace is a good starter for a collection of cushion types, with its willingness to grow and bloom without too much demand on the cultivator's time and skill. In this respect it is very rewarding, making an attractive plant with flowers generously produced

8. A 'snowball' of flowers describes *Androsace vandellii* at its best.

and held a little way above the cushion, singly, on pale green stalks. The petals are somewhat rectangular and a flawless white.

An interesting facet of behaviour is the manner in which, when the flowers are spent, their stalks bend over to lay the developing seed heads on the surface of the cushion, to look like little writhing worms. If this strange thing is done to aid seed dispersal, then how it does so is a mystery.

Androsace vandellii

How fitting that the final species to be introduced should be, from a grower's viewpoint, perhaps the ultimate cushion androsace. Over the years it has had at least four names, one of which (*A. argentea*) referred to the silver sheen of its cushion foliage. This is but one of its attributes; the others are its abundance in flowering, the fine symmetry of its cushion, a good resistance to pests and diseases, and a strong determination to stay in character. As if these were not

9. A colony of *Androsace vandellii* on a raised bed.

enough, *A. vandellii* is alone in being the androsace which can actually be grown bigger and flower better in cultivation than in the wild. What more could we ask?

Judged by its unusual distribution, this species must be old, in evolutionary terms. The fact that it is found in the Alps, the Pyrenees, and the Sierra Nevada (in southern Spain) suggests that it has survived major geological and climatic events in these high refuges. By nature it is a truly saxatile plant, growing only on granite cliffs and apparently indifferent to whether or not its selected niche is shaded or in the sun, provided that the roots can find dependable sources of moisture. The flowers can be so crowded that they often overlap, smothering the cushion in a white froth. On one memorable occasion the flowers on a particularly fine culti-vated specimen were carefully counted: the perfect, hemispherical cushion, 17 cm

(7 in) across, bore 2200 flowers, all open at the same time.

Successful cultivation requires nothing excessive in the way of treatment or provi-sion, if it is accepted that at no time should plants be exposed to rain or over-head watering. Youngsters will tolerate summer showers, but after their first year should be put with the adults under permanent cover. It is probably wise to provide some shade in mid-summer, if only to slow down moisture loss from the exceptionally lean soil mixtures that best suit this androsace. In very dry areas the mixture that follows might need some additional moisture-retentive material, but a well-tried and safe blend to try initially is, by volume, one part leafmould to two or even three parts of non-limy grit. Obviously the nutrients in such mixtures are quickly depleted and potting-on will be necessary at least annually.

If for any reason you can grow only one androsace or are trying them for the first time, choose this one.

Flowering times

For good reasons, no mention has so far been made of when the various species can be expected to flower. In the case of the cultivated plants there would have been tedious repetition, as all those mentioned bloom at some time during the five or six weeks from the end of March to early May. Wild plants respond to changes which are dependant upon the climatic trends in any particular year. Alpine guides will confirm that there are early and late springs in the mountains which can advance or delay the responses of the plants there by as much as a month. Hence the best that can be said is that flowering will take place in spring.

The hybrids

Some strange marriages have been contrived by growers curious to see what manner of offspring might result from bringing together species which could never cross in nature. Interestingly, the most successful hybrids arise from liaisons that could and sometimes do occur in the wild, where the territories of the two species involved approach within pollinating distance or even overlap. But not all of the natural crossbreeds take to a life in exile; there are some which occur regularly in the mountains, yet as cultivated plants are much more difficult to satisfy than either of their parents. The notes which follow concern only those hybrids that have proved to be amenable in cultivation and are worthy in their own right. There are but three:

A. carnea × A. pyrenaica

The pink of *A. carnea* often tints the flowers of this very variable hybrid and the influence of both parents can produce anything from single blooms to multi-flowered umbels, usually on stalks much shorter that those of *A. carnea*. The leaves and cushions can tend towards either parent, but are rarely out of proportion. Unless unusually lucky, the grower will need to raise many seedlings in the search for outstanding forms and to this end hand-assisted cross-pollination of the two species is helpful.

A. cylindrica × A. hirtella

No need to assist these two in their interactions; left within pollen reach of each other they will produce copious seed. That which is harvested from *A. hirtella* rarely comes true, but will give rise to a brood of delightful mongrels, with hardly a one that is not at least as attractive as its parents. *A. cylindrica*, on the other hand, must have superior genes, for although an equal partner in the pollen exchange, a good proportion of its seed can be expected to remain valid.

In its selected best forms this hybrid is superb, being amongst the easiest of the androsaces to please and the equal of the finest in character and appeal.

A. × marpensis

A new and vigorous hybrid that has come to us only very recently; it was found as a natural cross in the wilds of Nepal, the parents being *A. muscoidea forma longiscapa* and *A. globifera*. Its rosettes are very similar to those of the former, but the flowers have the form, habit and colour of the latter: almost sessile, often single and of a clear lilac with a yellow eye. As yet the plant can only be persuaded to flower in a restrained manner, but the growth is lusty and rapidly builds up a fat cushion. A rich, non-limy scree is presently sustaining

10. **Dianthus on a dry mountain flank in Turkey.**

good plants, and it is also succeeding as a pot-grown specimen in a half-and-half compost. Full light is essential if the cushion is to remain compact and flower well, plus plentiful watering or openness to the rain in spring and summer. However, overhead cover in the resting season must be provided, otherwise the whole cushion will quickly succumb to fungal disease and rot.

Availability of androsaces

In this respect, unless a special note has been added to a particular species description, it should be taken that the plant can be obtained from one or other of the specialist alpine nurseries, or that seed is in good supply.

THE DIANTHUS

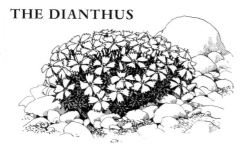

Although greater in number than the drabas, the *Dianthus* species have evolved with nothing like the same wanderlust. The heaviest concentrations are on the Balkan peninsula and from that nucleus restrained migrations have gone east and west. As a race they are predominantly sun-lovers, with a marked preference for limestone regions, though there are woodland and shade-seeking types. Only a moderate proportion of the species can be classed as Alpine, for although rocky ground is the commonest of their habitats, it is more often in foothills and even along coastal formations than on lofty ridges or summits.

Whereas the word 'cushion' is frequently but loosely used to describe the habit of many species, better adjectives might be 'tussock' or 'tuft', as so many of the *Dianthus* produce a grassy mat or hump. Only a very few develop a cushion which satisfies the definition arrived at in Chapter 00 and it is from these that the species to be introduced have been chosen.

As the advice on cultivation is common to all, it can be presented as part of this introduction. The preference of *Dianthus*

for light soils has already been mentioned and for most of them a significant lime content is a benefit. A loam of reasonable quality, mixed with an equal amount of grit, is quite satisfactory and any fertilizer supplement should be minuscule, otherwise the resultant growth will be rank and the flowers few; if in doubt, leave it out! Open, sunny sites sheltered from cold winds are the ideal, but it should be remembered that these dry out quickly and the *Dianthus* are not equipped to survive drought. Troughs, screes and raised beds are excellent planting places and unless the local winters are exceptionally wet, there is no need for overhead protection. Aphids have a great appetite for the sap of young shoots and should be strictly controlled. Propagation is straightforward, either from seed, which is usually set quite generously, or from cuttings taken as non-flowering shoots in July. The availability of plants from nurseries is normally good.

Flowering times

A great asset of the *Dianthus* species is their relatively late flowering time in the rock garden, which begins when most alpines are well past their zenith and busy developing seed heads. Late May–June–July is the period when the cheerful pinks, whites and rose hues can be expected, if the year is anything like normal in pattern. They extend the interest and impact of beds and troughs, and if a few silver saxifrages are included in the plantings, their graceful white plumes will rise at the same time to contrast with the bright discs of the *Dianthus*.

Dianthus alpinus

There was, admittedly, some hesitation in including this dianthus, because it is undoubtedly on the borderline between cushion and mat, and which of these forms it adopts is dependant on where it

grows. On the high moorlands of the Austrian Alps it definitely creeps along, but in rockier habitats, in the Styrian mountains, and also in the garden, it can compress its growth to an acceptable bun. Its cheerful inconsistency includes the colour and pattern of the flowers, which may be carmine with a purple centre in one form and unmarked pastel pink in another. They can sit almost stemless on the foliage or be raised on stout, leafy stalks, sometimes deeply infused with the pigment of the petals. *D. alpinus* has been a great favourite with rock gardeners from the very early days and needs little in the way of care and attention, being easily raised from seed, which is unstintingly produced, or from cuttings. The latter, taken as non-flowering shoots in summer, root easily and within months make vigorous youngsters ready for planting out. With such assets how could it be excluded?

In its cushion form the plant makes a good solid mound of its strap-shaped, glossy leaves in open and interlaced rosettes, from the centres of which rise the relatively huge flowers, putting a roof of colour over the whole leafage. If there is a failing it is in the short life of the garden plant, which after two or three years may simply expire or, as is more often the case, linger on, becoming more and more wasted and bedraggled. There is little profit in trying to reverse the decline when replacements can be raised so easily. Scree beds are rather too lean for this dianthus; its growth and flowering are best when the roots are in a very well-drained, limy, wholesome soil containing about 50% grit. Shade will seriously reduce the quantity and quality of flowers – to none at all if too dense. Buy the plant or beg the cutting when the flowers are there to see, otherwise the eagerly

11. *Dianthus erinaceus* in a sunny raised bed.

awaited display may not be what was expected; the variations include some poor flower forms and some harsh colours.

Dianthus erinaceus

In a small, immaculately-kept garden in north-west England there is an old specimen of this dianthus which, over many years, has made a 'pillow' big enough for a king-sized bed, but in all its long life it has never produced a single flower. Not all clones have this complete reluctance, though none could win praise for wealth of bloom, but the best forms will put up a respectable covering of the short-stemmed, pink flowers with attractively fringed petals. The real strength of the plant is in its cushion – a mounded pad of prickly, glaucus-grey foliage, immaculate throughout the year and certain to capture the attention of any garden visitor. Any of those visitors with the irritating habit of poking or patting cushions will do so only once: D. erinaceus has the retaliation of a hedgehog.

For obvious reasons it is wise to select purchased plants when they are in flower.

Alternatively, grow on a batch of seedlings and enjoy your own freedom of choice.

Dianthus freynii

It was a long time before all the arguments were settled and D. freynii was officially recognized as a distinct species. It inhabits the hills around Hercegovina and very slowly makes a compact, rounded cushion of small, blue-grey leaves which are a perfect foil for the petite pink or white flowers. Like many slow-growing plants it is long-lived and as a trough subject will never be a threat to its neighbours or overreach the allotted space. Gritty, limy soil, good drainage and a place in the sun which does not suffer from parching will keep this little gem content for a decade or so.

There may be difficulties in obtaining the true plant from commercial sources. There are imposters around that might be hybrids or even other species wrongly labelled. Seed should be from a reliable source, such as a collection made from wild plants by qualified people; garden-harvested seed is always suspect due to the wayward behaviour of Dianthus in cul-

tivation: they delight in exchanging genes. Cuttings root easily and ensure true reproduction.

Dianthus haematocalyx

There are two forms of this mountain species, and it is the high altitude *D. h.* ssp. *alpinus* that has the appeal for the cushion plant grower. One of its haunts is on Parnassus, but it is also to be found on peaks and ridges elsewhere in Greece and other limestone ranges in Eastern Europe. The low cushion is a hedgehog of blue-green, sharply pointed leaves, and it holds its eye-catching appearance through all the seasons. During the floral jamboree of the spring rock garden the cushion lies at rest, with not a bud to be seen, but then in late

12.   The wild dwelling-place of *Dianthus microlepis*, in Bulgaria. (A. M. Edwards)

June and early July comes a sudden rising of short flower stalks, each with a single swollen calyx stained blood red. Soon the flowers unfold to present their wedge-shaped, ragged-edged petals, which are burgundy on their upper surfaces and a creamy buff beneath. A healthy, well-placed plant will almost hide its cushion with flower.

A lean scree is a little too spartan for this species; it prefers rockwork in which it can root down into light, limy soil containing reasonable food supplies and with first class drainage. It should not be deprived of any sun, otherwise its compactness will degenerate and its flowers will be few. In tufa it is slow; perhaps too slow, for the growth tends to become stunted and woody, and the flowers dwindle. As a pot plant it is well behaved and can be grown to immaculate standards, given a compost something like the half-and-half blend, and plenty of light. In all respects this is a hardy plant, needing no form of shielding, but aphids and ants can be damaging (see Chapter 6). It is said that the seed set by cultivated specimens of *D. haematocalyx* comes true, which is very unusual for this genus, but to be absolutely sure of reproducing a good clone the safest method of increase is by cuttings, taken in late July or August. The plant is not at all common in nursery stocks, but there are a few to be found in the specialist nurseries.

Dianthus microlepis

In general appearance and behaviour *D. microlepis* is so like *D. freynii* that when the two are grown side by side it requires detailed examination to differentiate between them. It is only by growing the two species that a difference becomes apparent which is hidden from the eye, for *D. microlepis* seems to have little taste for lime. It responds better to neutral or even slightly acid soils in cultivation, though

13. *Dianthus microlepis* in person. (A. M. Edwards)

14. Aubrietas are too well known to need description, yet in nature are very localized and little seen, in the wilds of south-east Asia. (R. Rolfe)

these still need a gritty, open structure and excellent drainage. The mountains of southern Bulgaria are home to this very choice dwarf, where it grows on rock and in rubble, seeking no shade from the sun. It is variable in the intensity of its flower colouring and some especially attractive forms have of late been raised from seed and are offered by one or two nurseries.

Slow growth and miniature stature, together with a welcome hardiness in all our weathers, make *D. microlepis* a perfect tenant for a trough and also a good pot-grown specimen for exhibition. There are no particular ills or foes that are unusually destructive, but it is well to remember that a few bites from a large slug or snail can devastate a diminutive cushion and only the grower can protect it from these vegetarian gluttons.

Obtaining plants should not prove difficult if the lists of appropriate nurseries are carefully searched when they are newly issued. With regard to increasing garden plants, the advice is identical to that given for *D. freynii*.

Dianthus pavonius (syn. *D. neglectus*)

As a rock garden plant *D. pavonius* goes back a long way, and for the most part under its old name of *D. neglectus*, a strange specific which apparently refers to its being 'insignificant when not in flower'. It is no less significant than other species in their bloomless state, and we are left wondering why this particularly fine plant was singled out for such a doleful name. For once the change is welcome. In cultivation its reputation varies, with some growers regarding it as fickle, yet in certain gardens it simply goes on getting larger and staying in the best of health. A mistake that can dampen its spirits is to assume that, like so many of the 'pinks', it will feel at home with lime-stone, for although it can survive alkaline soils, it is principally a plant of non-cal-careous ground. At the lower altitudes of its locations in the French Alps it mingles with the short turf overlying granites and acid schists, but there it is of coarser, looser growth than on the heights, where it makes concise and densely-packed cushions of its grass-like foliage. The flowers of the high-level types sit close to the leaves, hiding the fawn undersides of their rose-pink petals until they close for the approach of bad weather, or at the ending of the day's sunshine.

It pays to be very selective when seeking a nursery plant or seed, as the compact and richly-flowered high alpine forms stay true to character in cultivation, and are worth hunting for. Provided that it is given the right start in garden life *D. pavonius* needs little attention thereafter, and should live for many years. A deep but lean and gritty soil in full sun is sufficient; anything richer, or shadier, will worsen its character. The sharp drainage of a raised bed, or a trough of good depth, will prevent the over-wet state at the roots which the *Dianthus* species dislike so much.

The hybrids

The creation of dianthus hybrids has occupied gardeners, both as a hobby and a serious commercial undertaking, for centuries, evident in the many 'carnations' and 'pinks' of the beds and borders. To a much lesser extent crosses have been contrived with the dwarf species to produce hybrids more suited to the rock garden, amongst which are some attractive cushion types. Newcomers appear from time to time, but are doubtful improvements on those which are already established. Examples are:

D. × boydii

A compact, bright-green dome bearing fringed flowers of cool pink with a darker centre. Blooms in July.

D. 'Elf'

A silver-grey hummock, putting up rather long stems to carry the semi-double flowers of rose pink. An unusually long flowering period of July to September.

D. 'Little Jock'

A double form, flowering pale pink on moderate stems in early summer. The cushion is a compressed tuffet of dove-grey, pointed leaves.

15. The ice-cream pink display of *Dianthus* 'Rivendell'. (S. Taylor)

D. 'La Bourbille'

Makes a neat grey-green cushion with wide-petalled white or pink flowers on short stems in June–July.

THE DIONYSIAS

If the androsaces are the aristocrats of the cushion plants, then the dionysias have to be of the royal line. They are unsurpassed in the pristine display of their flowers and the absolute compactness of their growth, added to which they bloom in yellows, pinks, icy blues and violets. Like the androsaces, they are closely related to *Primula* and have evolved along similar lines, reducing height and leaf size to become, in many instances, the exquisite buns of clustered leaves and flowers that captivate all who see them. Others in the family are more lax in character, but all are classified by the botanists as dwarf shrubs. The primary feature which puts them into this category is the behaviour of their stems, which over the years develop into woody branches, though these may be hidden by the dense canopy of foliage in the cushion forms. Cultivated dionysias seldom, if ever, live long enough to attain this mature characteristic.

The main concentrations of *Dionysia* are in the mountains of Iran and Afghanistan, and there are further but sparser locations in south-eastern Turkey, northern Oman, the Pamirs and Pakistan. Shaded and semi-shaded cliffs and rocks are the habitats sought by the majority of species, often in gorges and chasms, with some favouring overhangs or cave entrances, where they are even found growing upside-down in ledge and roof crevices. Many of the sites are in areas of limestone or limestone conglomerates similar in appearance and texture to tufa. The moisture supplies are obvious whilst there is melting snow around or spring

16. Dionysias light up the very early spring in the alpine house.

rain falling but later, in the dehydrating summers, the sources are not apparent and something of a mystery. Naturally, the desert region species are accustomed to a hot, dry atmosphere in the middle months of the year, but the winters in these and the other locations are severe. Consequently the dionysias are no strangers to dramatic annual temperature ranges.

Sadly, political upheavals and war have terminated our access to a great many of the habitats, leaving our studies of the plants incomplete. It is strongly believed that there are still new species of *Dionysia* to be discovered in these now forbidden territories. It may be many years before exploration can be resumed. Lacking access to the wild plants, we are totally reliant on existing cultivated stock for sustaining the species. In many instances seed is very difficult or impossible to coax from the plants in our care and cuttings are the sole means of increase.

Much has still to be learned about the cultivation of dionysias, even though remarkable progress has been made in the last ten years or so. Collections of any size are still only in the hands of a few dedicated growers, all of whom strive continuously both to improve their own success and to make more species available. With just a few exceptions, whose needs are comparable to those of the choice androsaces, the dionysias are undoubtedly among the most difficult of all alpine plants to grow and maintain. There are interesting contrasts in the methods employed by those growers who have achieved recognized expertise, showing as usual that there is no unique procedure involved in the successes and no 'absolutely essential' materials employed. The basic treatment in the cultivation of dionysias is the same for all the species with which we shall be concerned and can, therefore, be advised at this stage (rather than repetitively adding it to each species description).

Soil mixtures have their customary aura of alchemy and mystique, every expert's being different, but each is the result of careful trials and is proven by positive results. Hence, in the reader's best interests, a fair, representative selection of the mixtures currently in use now follows. All ingredients are in volumetric measures.

(a) 1 part J.I. No. 2, 1 part stone chippings (3 mm), 1 part coarse sand. Widely used and easy to prepare.

(b) 1 part sphagnum peat, 1 part coarse sand, 1 part sterilized loam, 3 parts stone chippings (2–5 mm). Similar to (a) in basic make-up.

(c) 3 parts stone chippings (3 mm), 1 part crushed tufa, 1 part perlite, 2 parts of mixed leafmould and loam (both sterilized).

(d) Equal parts of: coarse sand, perlite*, vermiculite*, stone chippings (2–3 mm) and J.I. No. 2.

NB: for details of John Innes compost, see page 106.

The essentials of cultivation are summarized below. Any special points about particular species are included in the individual descriptions.

(1) Very few of the cushion dionysias will tolerate any wetting of the foliage. With one or two exceptions they are really only suitable for alpine house culture, where they seem actually to appreciate the hot, dry conditions that prevail in the summer months.

(2) Some shading from direct sun is necessary, but at other times, when there is cloud or haze, the plants should be given full light.

(3) Botrytis mould is the foremost enemy of dionysias, and every means should be employed to dispel dampness and humid air.

(4) All successful growers agree that overwatering not only encourages moulds, but is also the principal cause of other terminal afflictions. It is safer

always to water by partial immersion of the pot, rather than to pour water round the rim, however carefully this is done.

Other than in storm conditions, or when there is a risk of in-blown snow, the ventilation of the alpine house should be maximized throughout the year. The effects of fog are excluded from this advice and will be discussed in a later chapter.

Dionysias seem impervious to frost. Temperatures as low as -25°C (-13°F) have had no apparent detrimental effects on cultivated plants.

The base of the cushion must be separated from the 'soil' surface by a layer of stone chippings or flakes, at least 2 cm (¾ in) deep.

Spent flowers should be removed to reduce the risk of mould attacks.

A close inspection for evidence of aphid infestation should be carried out at least weekly and treatment applied at the first signs.

Leaf rosettes which are wilting, progressively yellowing or have the slightest touch of mould must be promptly removed.

Although it has been necessary to stress the difficulties attending the cultivation of these challenging plants, the reader should not be intimidated by them. There are sufficient instances of growers with limited experience producing triumphs that have startled the experts, to encourage anyone with the urge to try.

All the species that follow are similar in general character, with neat, compact cushions and blooms resembling those of the primrose, except for the much-extended corolla tube, which is the striking feature of many *Dionysia* flowers.

---

* Perlite and vermiculite are expanded forms of volcanic rock and mica, respectively.

17. Impressive skill is required to produce superb specimens of the extra-difficult *Dionysia afghanica* (top).

18. A well-grown pan of *Dionysia archibaldii*.

Dionysia afghanica

Here is a species with a happy ending to its perilous story, for it could not possibly have come closer to the edge of extinction in cultivation. A few seeds were gleaned from the crushing of dried plant fragments collected in the wild, half a dozen of which germinated and just two of these seedlings grew on to become small specimens. Unfortunately these were subsequently lost and the sole survivor was a rooted cutting taken from one of them before its demise. Due entirely to the dogged determination of one highly skilled grower, that single rosette was coaxed into becoming a healthy plant; the source of all *D. afghanica* in UK (and almost certainly worldwide) cultivation, at the time of writing.

D. afghanica is found only in the Darrah Zang Gorge of north-western Afghanistan, on semi-shaded limestone cliffs, frequently beneath overhangs or in cave entrances, where it grows just as well upside-down as it does on vertical rock faces. The location is by no means arid: the lower reaches of the gorge are quite well populated by trees, shrubs and herbs. Furthermore, there are other species of *Dionysia* sharing the habitat.

In nature and in cultivation this is a slow-growing species, making a firm cushion of dark green, sticky leaves, which it covers in early spring with a mass of closely-held flowers of a pleasing light lilac hue. The corolla tube is typically long and at its mouth is an intense violet, giving the flower a sharp, dark eye. The plant's zest for blooming is such that it is usual for every rosette to produce a flower and even infants can be expected to do the same. From that which has already been said, it will be obvious that the only means of increase is to take single leaf-rosettes as cuttings. Although this species is of the more difficult to please in cultivation, it has become increasingly available from specialist nurseries over the past few years.

Dionysia archibaldii

When the first introduction of this species was made in 1966 the seed-raised plants were of two types. One was generously covered in farina and of a lax, shrubby habit; the other was described as a cushion-former lacking any farina. The latter dwindled until it was feared lost to

cultivation, but then reappeared in seedlings derived from the surviving shrubby types. The two are now safely established in cultivation and clearly distinguished as the 'farinose form' and the 'efarinose form'. After some investigation at the time of writing it was confirmed, by some healthy and mature examples, that *D. archibaldii* 'efarinose form' will consistently produce a well-shaped and compact cushion, and that it can be sustained as an adult plant using the methods developed for the culture of dionysias under glass.

If this species has a fault it is its very early flowering, which takes place in February and sometimes sooner if the winter is mild. It blooms more modestly than many of the other species, with long-tubed corollas of a light violet enhanced by golden eyes. The foliage is rather soft and made up of slightly loose rosettes, the curled leaf edges clearly featured. This is certainly one of the more difficult dionysias to grow and maintain, succumbing quickly to botrytis if conditions are not very carefully controlled. It appreciates regular watering in the warmer months, but during autumn and winter requires a just-moist compost. The biggest problem arises if February brings hard frosts when the plant is trying to flower and needs reliable moisture supplies at its roots, calling for special efforts by the grower to prevent the pot from freezing.

Two or three specialist nurseries offer this form fairly regularly. The plants may originate from propagation by cuttings (which are not at all easy to root), or from seed set on cultivated specimens.

Dionysia aretioides

In this robust and undemanding species we have the exception that proves the rule. Willing and rewarding in cultivation, it grows quickly and flowers abundantly, needing only a roof over its head in the colder, wetter months and if this is provided, even by a simple pane of glass, *D. aretioides* can even be planted in a trough or raised bed with good expectations. Why it should be so amenable compared to others in the genus is something of a mystery. The natural habitat has no significant differences to those of its relatives: it lives in the Elburtz mountains of Iran on the limestone cliffs of high valleys and there are no unusual aspects to the local climate. The wild plants are quite variable with a conspicuous division into farinose and non-farinose forms. Both of these produce smoothly-rounded and somewhat soft cushions, generously covered, in early spring, with 'primrose' flowers ranging through soft lemons to rich butter yellows. Several selected clones have been introduced since it was first collected in 1959, chosen for various merits of compactness, flowering and foliage.

The natural vigour of the species is almost too much for pot culture, in which it really needs to be moved on to a larger size twice in each growing season for the best results. Consequently, after a few years, the plant can present its owner with a definite risk of muscular injury if the pot has to be moved! Propagation is straightforward, either by cuttings or seed, the latter being regularly available, thanks to the plant's obliging fertility in cultivation. No fuss is involved in the preparation of soil mixtures, the only essential being excellent drainage. Water should be freely supplied in the growing season and not too sparingly during dormancy, otherwise the plant may never awake to greet the following spring. Another method of cultivation not yet mentioned is to plant a healthy infant in a block of tufa; this will restrain its gusto to some extent with no curb to its other functions. Whatever the method, *D. aretioides* should be grown, if just for the sheer pleasure of owning such a magnificent cushion plant.

Dionysia bryoides

Definitely to be counted as one of the most difficult to cultivate, but of such charm that it deserves every effort to keep it alive. If the plant can be persuaded to survive the winter it will almost certainly flower, and with such closeness that the petals touch and overlap to roof the cushion with bright, pink bloom. The centre of each flower has a pronounced zone of white or very pale yellow, giving a sparkle to the whole floral show. The individual leaf-rosettes are small, tight and closely packed, creating a dense and firm dome, but whereas the wild plants eventually become bare-branched at the base, cultivated specimens are very unlikely to live long enough for this symptom of age to develop. Countering the short life expectancy is the zest of this species to flower well when very young; a thumbnail-sized juvenile in full bloom can have a very special appeal in its petite and immaculate display.

A surprising element of the plant's history is that it was introduced (as seed) in the earlier days of alpine gardening, as long ago as 1932. There are no records of any survivors and it was not until 1966 that a new collection was returned. A further introduction in the early 1970s brought other clones into cultivation and all today's stocks have their origins in those two sources. In its infancy *D. bryoides* can be deceptively easy to maintain, but disaster, in the form of fungal attack, can strike with astonishing suddenness, mortally afflicting the plant in a single day. The most effective defence that the grower can employ is the routine taking and raising of cuttings, as insurance against this ever-present threat.

Dionysia curviflora

The undisputed record holder for permanence in cultivation, having been sustained since its original introduction in

19. Although normally a plant of acid rocks, *D. curviflora* is content on tufa, in cultivation (top).

20. A show-winning specimen of *D. curviflora*. (R. Rolfe)

1932 to the present day. Descendants from the first seed-raised plants are still being grown and it says much for the optimism and determination of enthusiasts that they have persevered even though those early clones were and still are rarely and thinly flowered. More eager flowering forms have come to us over the past twenty years or so and can now be obtained with little trouble.

In terms of difficulty *D. curviflora* is rated as one of the easier species, though it still requires regular attention and year-round residence in the alpine house. The cushion is only moderately humped and whilst it can be of near-perfect symmetry, it is more often met with as a curiously sculptured shape, an effect created by emergency surgical operations made necessary by attacks of botrytis. As usual, this scourge is the major problem for the grower, but in the case of *D. curviflora* is less likely to have terminal effects. The removal of mould-affected chunks from the cushion will often halt the spread of the affliction, provided that the amputation includes not only the obviously blighted leaf-rosettes, but also any which are, to the slightest degree, suspect. It is these cutting-out operations that alter the cushion's profile, yet they seldom cause permanent disfigurement, as once rid of its ailing parts this very forgiving dionysia can quickly recover and produce new growth to cloak the scars. Well-cared for plants can live for many years and may be up to 25 cm (10 in) across. Although the flowers are rarely so densely borne that they smother the cushion, the best clones put up a good display in a range of pleasant pinks and violets, with the corolla eye varying from pale to deep yellow.

Unlike so many in the genus, *D. curviflora* favours acidic rocks, its known habitats being on volcanic formations in the mountains of Iran, where it seeks full or partial shade on crags in the 3000–4000 m (9000–12000 ft) altitudes.

Dionysia freitagii

A stroke of good fortune attended the first raising of this species from seed collected by two quite separate expeditions in 1971. The plants grown included both pin- and thrum-eyed flowering forms, thus providing the essential differences for successful pollination and the possibility of home-grown seed. All went well and the carefully nurtured specimens produced viable seed, making the future of *D. freitagii* in cultivation much more secure. Where increase by cuttings was tried the plant was less helpful, the single leaf-

rosettes being very prone to rotting before any roots could form. A success rate of anything above 5% is still regarded as an achievement and trials are regularly carried out in search of improvements.

As well as being an exceptionally fine species, *D. freitagii* is somewhat less vulnerable to mould attacks in cultivation than other choice types. The cushion is a firm cluster of rather sticky, prominently-veined leaves, atop which sit the closely-spaced flowers. The petals are a cool mauve, deepening to a rich violet at the base to form a darker halo around the yellow eye. The blooms are never so crowded that they hide the cushion, but are plentiful and long-lasting, appearing very early in the year (late January–early February) unless the winter is unusually cold. Availability is now fairly good although still restricted to specialist nurseries.

The wild plants are confined to mountains in North Afghanistan where they inhabit shaded limestone cliffs, flowering later than their cultivated brethren, in April or May.

Dionysia involucrata

As a cushion there is nothing really extra-ordinary about this dionysia: the leaf-rosettes and leaves are a little larger than average and the cushion takes a year or two to consolidate, but otherwise it conforms to the expected shape and behaviour – until it flowers. Then it breaks the pattern and sends up burly stems to carry loose umbels of bloom several centimetres above the foliage. Where the flowers (up to five) branch out from the top of the stem, leaf-like bracts form a large, conspicuous ruff and the whole display resembles a group of raised banners. In their youth the flowers are lilac-pink with

21. The dark-eyed, lilac flowers of *Dionysia freitagii*.

a clear white eye, but later the whole centre of the corolla deepens in tone to magenta.

For the cultivator the plants are hardly more demanding than the easy-going *D. aretioides* and can be propagated either by seed, which is reliably produced, or from cuttings. Flowering takes place later than it does in most dionysias and the plant is frequently seen among the exhibits at British April shows. Vulnerability to moulds is so much less in this species that it is well worth trying in a trough or in raised bed planting, with a glass cover for the resting period. Availability is good, due to the relative ease with which it can be increased by seed or cuttings.

The wild plant colonies are located in the mountains south of Samarkand and are localized on limestone cliffs facing north or north-west. As in cultivation, the flowering time is later than usual for dionysias, extending from May into June.

Dionysia janthina

In many ways *D. janthina* is very similar to *D. curviflora*; in fact, until the early 1960s, the two were even thought to be variations of the same species. There were reasonable grounds for this confusion, as both inhabit one particular mountain locality in Iran, but it is now established that whereas *D. curviflora* is a high-altitude dweller, *D. janthina* has never been found above the 2000 m (6500 ft) contour and chooses calcareous rock as opposed to the acidic types favoured by *D. curviflora*. Other distinguishing features of *D. janthina* are the comparative hairiness of its cushion and its very early (or very late?) flowering in cultivation, which can take place at any time from October to December.

The grower cannot go far wrong in treating this species and giving it the same conditions as *D. curviflora*. Unfortunately, only pin-eyed plants were raised from the collected material, hence there is little hope of further seed; cuttings remain the only means of increase. This is a beautiful and not overly difficult species to culti-vate, and when content can live for many years, brightening the drab days of the year with its posy of mauve-pink flowers.

Dionysia lamingtonii

Every dionysia introduced so far is found in partial or full shade in its natural dwelling places, an understandable response to the heat and the dehydrating airs that are characteristic of the regions where they live, but *D. lamingtonii* spurns the shadows and chooses rocks in full sun, even though its place, in the Zagros Mountains of western Iran, is no less hot or dry.

In its dormant state the hard, tight cushion has an alarming appearance: a dismal, brown hump that looks as though it has succumbed to drought some time ago, but this is normal. Unless the plant is in fact dead, careful examination of the leaf-rosettes will reveal a pinhead of green

nestling in each centre and hope is restored. These tiny points of life will swell to become the spring foliage, but before they are fully developed the flowers will rise, one from each rosette, to make a dome of golden yellow rivalling any floral display in the cushion plant world.

Surprisingly, despite its apparent brush with death every winter and its defiant sun-loving lifestyle, *D. lamingtonii* har-bours no extra problems for the cultivator. A very simple soil mixture, composed of J.I. No. 2 and an equal quantity of grit or fine chippings (such as limestone, granite, flint) has sustained prize-winning speci-mens for years, and the older these have become the more exuberant has been their flowering. The first successful intro-duction was made as recently as 1973 and is likely to be the last for some time, unless remarkable political changes take place. Thankfully there is, as yet, nothing precarious about the stay of this species in cultivation, although through lack of success in home-produced seed, cuttings are the one means of maintaining stocks. Young, vigorous shoots are necessary to

achieve rooting and must be taken from youthful plants, almost a case of cuttings from cuttings. March and April are the usual months when flowering takes place in cultivation, which is opportune for growers to exhibit this exquisite dionysia at the spring shows.

Dionysia michauxii

Some sixty years ago this species had a brief debut in cultivation, living long enough to form young specimens and to be exhibited, but it then failed. A second collection of seed, made in 1939, produced a few plants which were sustained for somewhat longer and through a time when the country was at war. Beyond 1944, however, their fate is unknown and we had to wait until 1966, when that tenacious plant-hunter Jim Archibald brought new supplies of seed. Since then *D. michauxii* has remained with us, though completely dependent upon propagation from cuttings for its continued existence. Now nursery-raised plants are available from time to time.

Of all the dionysias this one is perhaps the most splendid when seen blooming in its natural state, making at its best an almost globular cushion, closely and entirely covered by the massed buttercup-yellow flowers. The foliage is a grey-green and produces tight leaf-rosettes, densely packed together. There is only a single and very localized occurrence of this species in nature, on limestone crags in south-western Iran, where it populates crevices and fissures which are mostly shaded during the hottest hours of the day but often enjoy the morning sunshine.

The primary skill in keeping the plant alive and well is knowing when and how much watering is needed. At any time of the year the safest course is to err on the dry side, as the slightest excess of moisture at the root can cause irreversible damage. To ensure that the critical moisture level is never exceeded the majority of successful cultivators grow the plant in a clay pot, plunged to its rim in sand, and water only the plunge. By this means the soil ball receives water by absorption through the pot wall. Such an arrangement is typical of the care needed to even partially satisfy some of the choice dionysias.

Dionysia tapetodes

One of the most widely-grown and accommodating cushion species, enjoying a firm establishment in cultivation, due in no small part to having been introduced as seed several times and from several sites since 1958. Many forms are grown, mainly from home-produced seed, and show considerable variation in vigour, colour, farina and the will to live. Some are delicately perfumed when in flower.

A wide distribution in the wild suggests a well-developed adaptability in the

22. *Dionysia lamingtonii*, grown to perfection.

23. The yellow 'plaque' of *Dionysia tapetodes*, grown in tufa.

24. *Dionysia tapetodes* grown as a show plant. (R. Rolfe)

species, which might explain its generally good response to life in unnatural environments. It occurs in many locations, from north-eastern Iran through Afghanistan to the border of Pakistan, and colonizes the shaded crevices and overhangs of limestone formations. The plant forms a precisely shaped cushion of tidy leaf-rosettes, which can be an attractive apple-green in the non-farinose forms, and at the other extreme so covered with farina that the entire plant appears to have been dusted with golden pollen. The liberally-produced flowers are held stiffly upright on the cushion, presenting their little rounded stars on moderately long corolla tubes, in a range of clear yellows.

D. *tapetodes* is a good species for the beginner in dionysia growing and although subject to botrytis attack, like the others can often be saved by prompt removal of the affected rosettes. It grows relatively quickly and will set seed if pin- and thrum-eyed specimens are together, appreciating a little assistance from hand pollination for the best results. Choice forms can be propagated by cuttings, which usually root with few problems.

The remainder

There are other dionysias in cultivation, but the likelihood of their ever becoming available in the foreseeable future, even in very limited numbers, is so slim that to have included them for full description would have served little purpose. However, it is just possible that a dedicated grower, heavily smitten by the dionysias and determined to acquire the ultra-rare species, might beguile a friendly expert to part with one or two cuttings or seeds. For anyone with such ambition, the species omitted, which at the time of writing do exist in cultivation, albeit in extremely small numbers, are as follows:

D. diapensiifolia

Only just being maintained in cultivation.

D. microphylla

Not too hard to grow, but almost impossible to increase by cuttings, and seed is in very short supply.

D. viscidula

Notoriously difficult to keep alive and only precariously held in cultivation.

A final note on cultivation

The rooting of cuttings is so crucial to the continuance of so many species in our care that a few comments in this regard are warranted.

Regardless of when the plant flowers, the optimum time for taking cuttings seems to be May or early June, but where circumstances carry any possible risk of losing the plant then cuttings should be made from any still-healthy shoots, whatever the time of year. In caring for the rarer species it is prudent periodically to take one or two cuttings on a 'just in case' basis. Rooting substances vary from grower to grower; clean, sharp sand is the most prevalent, but pumice and, more recently, rooting gels have also brought successes.

Shading is an aspect of cultivation that is all too often badly defined, and as it plays an important role in the culture of dionysias, some clarification is needed.

Many dionysias seek shade in their natural habitats, but it should be appreciated that in the hot, dry regions where they occur the sunlight is harsh and shines from clear skies, day after day during the months when the plants are active. On the cliffs and in the gorges the light is reflected from the pale rock surfaces into the shaded parts, increasing the quality and level of illumination there. In consequence, although the plants are not in direct sunlight they are receiving light that is stronger and more consistent than that which they would get in, say, a position under the staging of an alpine house or a bed at the foot of a north-facing wall. In cultivation it is a case of tempering the direct light of our weaker northern sun and not putting plants into full shadow, where they will become drawn, weakened and disinclined to flower.

THE DRABAS

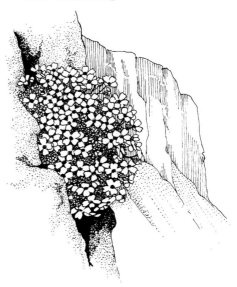

There are well over two hundred known species of *Draba* and the distribution is impressive; they occur from top to bottom of the American continents and span the whole of Eurasia, from Spain to Siberia. Although the great majority have a congested, tufted habit of growth, a large proportion of them fail to qualify as cushion plants, and of those that do, a considerable number have little to recommend them as subjects for cultivation. Even so, with all the non-cushion and lack-lustre types excluded, sufficient remain to put the drabas amongst the major cushion plant families in cultivation.

25. Crucifers do not get the attention they deserve.

Of the species selected for attention no more than a half dozen, which have remained popular with several generations of rock gardeners, are easy to obtain. The scarcity of the others is no reflection on their worth or their behaviour in cultivation, but has much to do with the fickleness of fashion. There does not seem to have been a heyday for the drabas; no time when any self-respecting rock gardener had to have a collection of them and an urge to grow every available species. Consequently, the less well known have appeared but fleetingly on the show benches and have only occasionally been featured in books and journals concerning alpine plants. Could it be, perhaps, that drabas have remained as 'Cinderellas' because they are crucifers? Some pundits of alpine lore have chosen to downgrade the crucifers generally, as though any flower with four petals were somehow inferior. Hopefully the descriptions which follow will help to right the wrong that has been done to plants deserving high regard.

In their cushions the drabas offer us subtle diversities of colour, texture and form: therefore those which grow heartily into real dumplings of fresh green, others that gradually build tight buns of almost grey leaves with a downy covering, and spiny-leaved little hedgehogs of sombre olive. The flowers may sit almost stemless on the cushion or be held in bunches on the slenderest of stalks.

With few exceptions the drabas are tolerant plants in cultivation, requiring no great precision or precious substances in the soil mixtures offered, and are less vulnerable to disease and adverse climate than their appearance might suggest. Most can be grown equally well as pot subjects or in troughs and beds, with simple, well-drained composts, such as: J.I. No. 2 (or good soil mixed with peat or leafmould) blended with an equal bulk of gravel or fine chippings. Just a few are only successful when grown as permanent residents of the alpine house or frame and these individuals will be identified in the descriptions. On the whole they are sun-lovers, but do need adequate moisture at the root. There are no particular difficulties in the raising of new plants from cuttings or seed.

Draba acaulis

A small and exquisite fluffy cushion which grows slowly and compactly on the high rocks of the Taurus mountains in southern Turkey. The grey-green, tightly clustered leaf-rosettes, with their covering of glistening hairs, give emphasis to the neat heads of golden-yellow flowers, which rise scarcely clear of the foliage. In and out of flower this species has a strong appeal for the enthusiast and is a test of

26. Drabas grow quickly to exhibition size if repotted regularly. (R. Rolfe)

skill almost equal to that posed by the dionysias. It is a plant needing full light to maintain its squat character and generous spread of flower, for which an open, sunny plunge bed is ideal in the spring and summer, but beware! Even when the plant is active it can be attacked by mould in extended wet periods and the wise grower will give it temporary cover until the weather improves. From early autumn until flowering is over (in the middle of the following spring) *D. acaulis* is safest in the alpine house, where the drier atmosphere and the grower's regular attention will help it through the most hazardous part of the year.

Special composts have produced no better results than a simple blend of 1 part J.I. No. 1 and 2 parts grit, but deep top-dressing, or shards of stone beneath the cushion are essential in the battle against fungal attack. Over-dry compost at any time and over-wet compost during dor-

mancy put the plant at risk, as do aphids (on foliage and roots) and the red spider mite.

Rarely is this species available from nurseries, but seed is sometimes listed and, if reasonably fresh, should germinate with little delay. Then comes the task of bringing the infants up to maturity; a slow process which, with some luck, will produce cushions of up to 5 cm (2 in) in diameter after three years.

Draba bryoides

The common form of the species is seldom seen in gardens or collections of pot-grown cushions, mainly due to the greater popularity of the variety *imbricata*, which is smaller in everything but flower. Both are native to the western Caucasus, growing on exposed, stony slopes at the Alpine levels. *D. bryoides* var. *imbricata* makes a tidy, moss-like, green mound of huddled leaf-rosettes, with no obvious hairiness. The yellow flowers are full-petalled and held in heads of up to five on very short stalks. The rather neglected basic species deserves more attention and appreciation; it forms a well-shaped cushion of close foliage and its flowers stand just clear of the leaf tips.

This is one of the easier drabas and can be grown in the open garden in scree-type beds, troughs or tufa. In a pot the plant is easily satisfied with a simple, well-drained compost. Winter wet may cause damage to the cushions of outdoor plants in some years and a basic overhead protector may be necessary. This plant is an exceptionally good subject for growing in tufa, where it can live to a great age (at least 20 years) and large size. The species, in its variety *imbricata*, is often in nursery stocks, but all too often grown in peat-based compost, which is difficult to remove from the very fine root system. Seedlings grow quickly and it is not unusual to have a mature plant after only three years. The growth

rate is much slower if the roots are confined to a tufa block.

Draba dedeana

The calcareous cliffs of the Spanish Pyrenees have their own very special flora, with a number of species which are not to be found anywhere else in the world, and included in these is *D. dedeana*. It makes a hardy and well-conformed bun of its dark green leaf-rosettes, which are bristly rather than hairy. The corymbs of white flowers are stubby and massed above the plant in early spring, on stems which increase in length to an eventual 5 cm (2 in), producing a succession of flowers as they do so. This replacement of fading blooms by freshly opening ones prolongs the flowering period, although towards its end the plant can take on a rather dowdy appearance with its litter of fallen petals and half-denuded stalks. Nevertheless, it is one of the foremost of the drabas in cultivation and tough enough for garden life if given a sharply drained perch. Lean compost induces compact growth and copious flowering in pot-grown plants, and similarly frugal mixtures should be used in troughs or beds. Although its hardiness is not in question, the best results are obtained from alpine house specimens, whose early blooms are neither battered nor soiled by wild weather.

This is a cushion plant that should be sought when it is in flower, or raised from seed for subsequent selection, as it is variable in growth and flower. Poor forms have rather scruffy cushions and flowers that incline to an undernourished look, with narrow petals and a greyish tinge in their colour. Seed, which is generally easy to obtain, can be expected to come true, as this is a species which does not hybridize readily. Growth is slow in the first year by draba standards, but speeds up later to give a cushion of some 10 cm (4 in) across after three seasons. The rooting of cuttings varies in success rate, being good in some years and poor in others. Aphids can be troublesome and well hidden in the rosettes.

Draba longisiliqua

In the time scales of plant introductions this species is a latecomer, collected for the first time by Western plant-hunters in 1976. Perhaps its location in the Russian Caucasus, delayed its discovery. The natural habitat is described as 'on lime-stone cliffs at 1500 m (5000 ft)', where it will certainly be hot in the summer months and which is possibly the reason for the grey, felty appearance of the leaves of *D. longisiliqua*, a feature of many plants subject to harsh drying conditions. In shape and composition the cushion is similar to that of *D. mollissima*, but the rosettes are larger and more open, giving a less smooth profile to the dome. In flower the plant has a mixed reception from rock gardeners; some take delight in the long and slender flower stalks flexing under the heads of yellow bloom, but others view the display as overloaded and out of proportion.

Probably due to its deceptively fragile appearance and the divided response to its floral character, this species is unlikely to become as widely grown as others in this section, but those who find interest and appeal are advised to grow the plant in the alpine house and to treat it in the same manner as *D. mollissima* or *D. polytricha*.

Draba mollissima

A consistent favourite with growers and fully deserving of its popularity, this Caucasian native makes a close and immaculate dome of velvety, fresh-green foliage. In early spring short, delicate stems extend to put a cloud of lemon-yellow flowers over the cushion, and their prominent stamens give a delightful fluffy effect to the whole display. It is an elegant plant

in all respects, and looks more difficult to please than it actually is.

In drier regions it can be grown as a garden plant, but exposure to the unkindnesses of winter gives rise to blemished and poorly-flowered cushions that compare badly with those kept in the shelter of the alpine house.

Provided that it is open and gritty, the compost for *D. mollissima* needs no exactness in its constituents; the half-and-half J.I. and grit mixture, or anything reasonably resembling it, is satisfactory. This is one of the more vigorous of the cushion plants; a seedling may reach 2.5 cm (1 in) across in only four or five weeks from germination. The root system is like a cobweb and very extensive, making it essential to pot up seedlings at an early stage and to repot them after another month or two if the young plant is not to be constricted and starved. From then on an annual repotting at the very least is necessary to the well-being of this draba. Lack of water will cause large-scale dying off of leaf-rosettes and even in dormancy the compost should remain moist, but even the most cared-for specimens are prone to sporadic fungal attack in winter, and any failing rosettes must be quickly removed. Shade will induce laxness in the cushion and little, if any, flowering. The craters left behind by extracted rosettes can be filled by gently levering neighbouring growth into modified positions.

Propagation by cuttings is quite easy, but there are interesting variations to be had from seed-raised plants, particularly in their inclination to flower. In addition to keeping a watch for mould a regular check needs to be made for aphids at all times of year, and for grazing slugs when mild, damp conditions prevail.

Draba polytricha

Another species from the mountains of eastern Europe and once described as 'the

27. *Draba polytricha* on the lofty limestones of north-east Turkey. (R. Rolfe)

classic alpine cushion plant'. Like so many of the genus it survives in a quite hostile climate, with intense cold in winter and periods of harsh, dehydrating sun and wind when it is in growth and flower. This is a tough plant with a deceptively vulnerable appearance to its soft, downy cushion, which might be mistaken for that of a high-altitude androsace. The stubby, bright yellow flowers are in crowded scapes, held quiveringly aloft on thin springy stems, capping the whole plant with a perfect hemisphere of bloom.

The culture is identical to that given for *D. mollissima*, and due to its similar popularity, it is to be found in most good alpine nurseries. Of all the drabas in cultivation *D. polytricha* is the one likely to live the longest and to grow to the greatest size; the limit is usually the weight of the pot and not the plant's capability to grow even bigger. Eight- to ten-year-old specimens will easily produce a beautiful symmetrical cushion of 30 cm (12 in) diameter and still oblige the grower with a mass of flower.

Draba rigida

A totally hardy species that competes with the best of the genus in quality and attractiveness, both in form and flower. Plant a well-rooted cutting or seedling in the face of a tufa boulder or a rock garden crevice and enjoy for the next ten to fifteen years the emerald-green cushion with its delicately-stemmed golden flowers. In such places *D. rigida* grows slowly as a tight mound of tiny, tufted leaf-rosettes and is seemingly impervious to sap-suckers, leaf-eaters and moulds. It may seed itself around in a restrained way and occasionally hybridize with other drabas in the vicinity, but on the whole the self-sown offspring will be true and ready to colonize any amenable cranny or scree within seed-blowing distance.

There is, from time to time, contention over this plant's name. It has been suspected of mixed parentage and has suffered demotion, on occasion, to a subspecies, but as it continues to be recognised as *D. rigida* despite the controversies, and as it is invariably labelled as such by nurseries, it is assumed innocent until proved otherwise.

Others

There are just a few more species in regular cultivation, but they are so like some of those already introduced that their descriptions and requirements would be almost exact repeats of the text. For example, *D. oligosperma* and *D. oreades* are very close in habit and appearance to *D. bryoides* and *D. mollissima*, although neither has quite the same flowering capability. There are more yellow-flowered soft-cushioned, and white-flowered spiny-cushioned types which make their debut, but then fail to persist, perhaps due to miffiness or the realization that they have not the quality to match the established species.

In American rock gardening the drabas are held in higher esteem than in Britain, and some thirty species are to be found in their plant and seed catalogues. They no doubt deserve this recognition, but there is a scarcity of descriptive information about them outside the USA ; we can only hope that this situation will soon be remedied, if only to show us what we are missing.

The hybrids

Drabas can and do hybridize, sometimes all too readily, and some strange plants have appeared on the show benches masquerading under the labels of true species, their owners unaware of the promiscuous acts taking place between their specimens. These mongrels rarely persist in cultivation, but there are two which are of such

merit that they have been maintained by vegetative propagation. The first of these arose from a crossing of *D. mollissima* with *D. polytricha* and was christened *D.* x *molytricha*; an unattractive name for what is a fine plant embodying the best of both parents. The second resembles a white-flowered *D. polytricha* and has been firmly in cultivation for many years; named *D.* x *salomonii* it gives no hint of its parentage.

THE RAOULIAS

Plants from the other end of the Earth, unique to large islands isolated for eons by great oceans; and yet, in their confined evolution, the New Zealand raoulias have reacted in the same way to the rigours of mountain life as have other genera in far-off continents, by compacting their growth into mats and cushions. But these cushions differ in more than one respect from those of the Old World, as will be revealed. They belong, together with the daisies, asters and many others, to the *Compositae*, though this is far from obvious when seeing the minute tuft-like flowers peeping through the foliage.

It might seem strange that cushion plants lacking any impact in floral display should be amongst those prized by keen growers of 'buns', but it is in the modelling and texture of their growth that the fascination lies; they have to be seen for their attraction to be fully appreciated. When they first came to us, and for some time after, we made the mistake of treating them in the same way as we did the difficult cushion types from other countries, giving them lean composts and the all-year protection of the alpine house. The terrain of their natural habitats and their vulnerable-looking downy foliage were our guides to their culture, but these were misleading and it was only when we obtained a more accurate and complete understanding of the conditions in the wild that we began to achieve some successes.

The home ground of the raoulias is high, bleak and rocky, snow-covered in the winter and exposed during the summer to periods of intense sunshine and drying airs, alternating with onslaughts from cold rain- and fog-laden winds. Some species root into cliff crevices, others into scree, with no apparent attempt to seek shelter from the harshness of the elements. In cultivation it was found, more or less by accident, that despite the frugal nature of their real-life rooting places, the plants improved greatly when given composts which, whilst free-draining, were high in fibrous and water-retentive material. Typical of these would be a blend of leaf-mould or peat, J.I. No. 1 and fine chippings or grit, in equal proportions. The heat and dryness of the alpine house in summer were, it was realized, a hindrance to the health and progress of the plants and startling improvements resulted from moving them out into plunge beds open to the weather. Only when late autumn brought long damp or wet periods of

29. The metallic-blue sheen on the foliage of *Raoulia bryoides*.

weather was it necessary to cover the cushions, keeping them dry as they would be under their mountain snow cover. This overhead protection is only required until March, when the raoulias begin to stir.

Perhaps due to some residual genetic memory, several *Raoulia* species continue to put on growth, albeit slowly, during the resting period (when it is summer in the Southern Hemisphere) and for this reason alone the roots should never be allowed to approach dryness. This is essential in any case for raoulias, as dehydration due to inadequate moisture in the compost is the most common cause of losses. They do fall prey, like many other cushions, to fungus attack and require the usual care and treatment in this respect, but the woolliness of their foliage is a deterrent to aphids.

28. Not a boulder, but a perfect dome of *Raoulia* (bottom right) in the mountains of New Zealand.

Raoulia bryoides

This species has the alarming habit of losing all its lustre in the autumn, turning a sickly grey and appearing lifeless through the winter. Not until early April is it possible to know whether the condition is permanent or merely a resting pallor; then, if all is well, the foliage comes alive again. Within a week or two the cushion is restored to its silver-grey sparkle, and new growth shows white at the centres of the rosettes.

Each leaf of the rosettes has a pelt of dense, short hairs, giving it the appearance of whitish-grey flannel and the rosettes cluster together in a shapely, soft cushion. The small flowers have a fawn-coloured centre surrounded by white bracts, but are rarely seen on cultivated plants in Britain.

The growth rate of this cushion is rather faster than those of the other species to be described, building a cushion some 12 cm (5 in) in diameter in four or five years from germination. A three-part compost, containing equal quantities of grit or fine chippings, J.I. No.1 and leaf-mould or peat, satisfies the plant's needs and as it becomes mature, a repotting every other year is sufficient. Being a crevice-dweller in nature R. *bryoides* is less vulnerable to fungus problems in winter if its cushion rests on flakes of stone rather than chippings. Single shoots are easily separated and snipped out for cuttings and there are no special problems to rooting them in moist sand in an ordinary propagator.

Raoulia buchananii

So compact and even are the honey-combed leaf-rosettes of this beautiful species that the whole cushion might be mistaken for a smooth head of sea-green coral. It is localized in New Zealand's Fiordland, where it dots the screes and

blooms with tiny red florets. The rubble surface upon which it is found in the wild gives no hint of its rooting requirement in cultivation, which is a compost that would not be amiss for a rhododendron: gritty enough for good drainage, but rich in leaf-mould and fibrous soil. The 'strong' compost, described in the chapter devoted to cultivation, is just about sufficient in humus-type content, yet a little more peat or leafmould could be added to it. R. *buchananii* is difficult to obtain and very averse to growing from cuttings. As it has yet to flower in cultivation (in the UK) the only real source is seed offered from authorized collecting in New Zealand.

Once established as a seedling it is in fact somewhat easier to please than other cushion raoulias. A sunny plunge bed, open to the weather of north-west

30. Some cushions are worth growing even though they may never flower in captivity (*Raoulia buchananii*).

England from spring to autumn, has kept one particular plant in good health and slow but unfaltering growth for several years now. The root system is scanty by comparison with most cushion species and repotting is only necessary at two-year intervals. Aphids and slugs pass it by, but parching will lead to serious if not fatal damage and winter rain will cause rot. Frost seems to have no ill effects and the plant can be left under cover in the plunge bed, where in mild winters it continues to add restrained but evident growth.

Raoulia eximea

As it passes from youth to adulthood R. eximea undergoes a change from the normal manner of growth for a cushion, and in a very strange way. The tap root, which it uses for initial anchorage and sus-tenance, is abandoned, together with the stems and withered leaves rising from it. Further growth roots down into this forsaken, peat-like mass of material for the remainder of the plant's life, and more material is added to the dead core as the plant continues to expand. The limit to the size that this process can create is presumably related to strength and stability, but wild plants of a metre and more across, and of great age, are not unusual. The cushion shape is more or less retained, although in large specimens there is some billowing which produces the appearance of a giant cauliflower head. Even in hot, dry periods the core is wringing wet and the surface shoots never want for moisture.

Such is the diminutive size of the flowers that they are insignificant, but this is more than compensated for by the cap-

31. *Raoulia eximea* on its native New Zealand mountainside.

tivating foliage. The leaf-rosettes are so compressed and so tightly packed that each takes the form of a blunted hexagon, with only the upper leaf edges visible. These are densely covered in fine hairs which bestow a silver-grey sheen to the 'skin' of the whole plant.

The chances of cultivated specimens reaching the change of growth stage are extremely slim. The size limit for plants in Britain is about 10 cm (4 in) across, at which stage they suddenly decline, perhaps because they want to make the change, but are unable to do so in the alien conditions. Not surprisingly, the compost used is highly fibrous and water-retentive; a successful make-up is 2 parts peat, 2 parts leafmould and 1 part grit. Good specimens have also been grown in proprietary peat-based, ericaceous compost. Little is needed in the way of supplementary nutrients and a tiny pinch of slow-release low-nitrogen fertilizer is sufficient for a litre (2 pints) of the compost mixture given. In nature the plants are found on stone-strewn slopes with a peaty sub-soil and the cushions sit on rock fragments. Accordingly, cultivated specimens should have a generous top-dressing beneath them, or better still flakes of stone. In the late autumn and winter the cushion will not tolerate wetness, but its roots must be maintained in a moist state. Any failing rosettes should be removed promptly and with great care, as they are so firmly connected to the cushion, and if plucked may bring away other healthy growth.

Young plants are periodically offered by specialist nurseries and seed is often available through rock gardening societies and clubs, both in Britain and abroad.

Raoulia mammilaris

A crevice-dweller which is to some extent a smaller-leaved and more compact version of R. bryoides; each rosette is fully expanded and so completely covered in fine down as to give the cushion an almost white appearance. In places it shares the same habitat with both R. bryoides and R. eximea and is concentrated in a district of the Canterbury Range in New Zealand. The flowers are of an inconspicuous fawn and have never been seen on captive plants in Britain. There is no shedding of original roots and growth by this species; it retains its deeply questing system for life and its rosettes are supplied from these through the ever-lengthening and branching stems in the conventional cushion plant manner.

Although living in the fissures of massive rock and presumably finding little soil or peaty deposits there, R. mammilaris does less than its best if given lean composts in cultivation. At least half of the constituents should be organic and moisture retentive if the plant is not to lose its enthusiasm for living after a short time. Of the cultivated species it is usually the slowest in rate of growth and rather more difficult to keep free of fungus problems in winter. Overhead cover is essential during its rest, but quite unnecessary whilst the plant is busy. In Britain a cushion which is anything more than 5 cm (2 in) across is an achievement, and at that size will represent three or four years of growth from the seedling stage, with one or two repottings. But the care and trouble are very worthwhile, for the cushion is one of the finest in the genus for symmetry and beauty.

Occasionally the smaller specialist alpine nurseries will list R. mammilaris and seed is periodically offered in the seed lists of rock gardening clubs and societies. Cuttings, taken as partially mature shoots, are not difficult to root or grow on.

32. **The bi-generic hybrid Raoulia x loganii enjoys full exposure to the weather throughout the growing season.**

Raoulia rubra

About once every ten years or so a small specimen of this species appears on the show benches, paying tribute to the seed-raising skill of its owner. Named for the red flowers it produces in nature, it is otherwise similar in growth and effect to *R. buchananii*, but with (in captivity) a greener hue to its cushion; it responds to the same treatment in culture. Sadly, the show bench debutantes never seem to make a second visit, which tells its own tale of survival, but we keep trying.

The hybrids

R. × loganii

The most outstanding and well established in cultivation is *R. × loganii*, which to be precise is not a true *Raoulia* hybrid but a bi-generic cross discovered as a natural occurrence. The parents are believed to be *Leucogenes leontopodium* and *Raoulia rubra*. It forms a splendid dense cushion of relatively large, broad-leaved rosettes bearing silvery hairs, and there is a glaucous-green cast to the foliage generally. Cultivation follows the same methods and course as that for *R. bryoides* and the plant is not difficult to keep. A good subject for a raised bed with winter cover, but equally responsive in a pot or trough.

Hybrid vigour is obvious in a contrived cross between *R. petraensis* (a mat-former) and *R. bryoides*, but other than for its superior growth rate, it is hardly distinguishable from the latter species, is no easier to please and rarely available.

Raoulia × petrimea

An excellent hybrid which has only lately come into circulation. Discovered in 1982 as a naturally-occurring cross between *R. petraensis* and *R. eximea*, where these two parent species share the same ground in the Grampian mountains of New Zealand's South Island. The common habitat lies at about 1500 m (5000 ft) on a north-facing (sunny) slope of wet, semi-stable scree.

The superbly uniform cushion is soft but densely packed, with chubby little rosettes of woolly leaves, closely resembling those of *R. bryoides*. There have been no reports of cultivated plants producing flower, but the blue-grey mound is well worth having on its own merit. Cultiva-

tion follows that for other cushion raoulias. A selected form of this hybrid has been given the cultivar name of 'Margaret Pringle'.

A note on seed

The seeds of the *Compositae* are not renowned for their ease of germination and those of *Raoulia* are in the more difficult category. Unless the collector is knowledgeable the seed may be missed altogether and the packets will contain only dry flower parts and chaff. Fresh seed gives undoubtedly better results and if it can be obtained from New Zealand quickly, then that which is collected in the autumn of the Southern Hemisphere arrives in the spring of our Northern Hemisphere – ready for immediate sowing.

Footnote

In the superb botanic garden of Gothenburg the cushion raoulias are grown to perfection under quite different conditions to those described above. The plants are in a large and lofty glasshouse equipped with winter temperature control and fan-assisted air circulation throughout the year. The compost used is extremely lean and gritty, enriched only by weak liquid feeding at regular intervals. At no time are the cushions exposed to the weather. No better example could be offered to emphasise the folly of regarding any one technique as the best and it should encourage braver growers to be ever open to new ideas and to devise and try out alternatives.

THE SAXIFRAGES

There are so many saxifrages! As a race they have been dubbed 'the backbone of the rock garden', and in any collection of cushion plants they can make an enormous contribution. Any attempt to present all of the cushion-forming species alone would swamp this section of the book and so the only realistic approach is to offer and describe a well-balanced selection. To help matters it is possible to

33. *Saxifraga* 'Duncan Lowe' is a fine form of *S. andersonii*.

divide them into three reasonably distinct groups, and because the hybrids within and between these are so widely popular, a fourth group can be dedicated to them. Hence the order of their introduction will be:

- The Kabschia Group
- The 'Silver' Group (sometimes called 'encrusted' types)
- The 'Mossy' Group
- The hybrids

The Kabschias

There are no exceptions or even border-line cases in this group; they are all true cushion plants and of marvellous variety. The typical Kabschia saxifrage is a hard bun of evenly-clustered leaf-rosettes and responds to the first stirrings of spring with a flush of superbly formed and vibrant flowers. The habitats are in the Old World, over the entire length of Eurasia and mostly at the lower, warmer levels of mountain regions.

Kabschias are often grown in pots, but not because they need to be; some bloom so early in the year that they can only be comfortably enjoyed in the alpine house or even (briefly) on the windowsill, hence the pot. But it is no kindness or advantage to keep such kabschias 'indoors' as spring progresses, for once their flowers are spent they are far better in an open plunge bed. Unless the garden is in a region of particularly high winter rainfall or subject to frequent periods of damp lifeless weather, kabschias can be grown in beds and troughs without any special treatment or devices. Places open to the sky but not broiled by the sun in summer will give them the high light levels necessary for compact growth and generous flowering, without the stresses of dehydration; perhaps by a rock which casts shade from late morning to mid-afternoon. Soil mixtures should be neither too rich nor too spartan. A reliable make-up, suited to most British conditions, would be equal parts of good loam, small stone chippings, leafmould (or peat) and grit. If a sound quality of J.I. No. 2 is available then, especially for potting, an alternative is to mix this with an equal bulk of coarse grit or small chippings. All the European species are from limestone terrain, but most of the Himalayans favour acidic formations and these opposing traits should be remembered in selecting materials for mixing.

A specialized branch of Kabschia culture is the growing of plants in tufa. These saxifrages are some of the most suitable subjects for this very striking mode of cultivation, which will be explained and discussed in a later chapter.

In the selection of species for description the aim has been to represent as fully as possible the differences in character within the kabschias, so that in effect the reader is provided with a good set of 'samples'.

Saxifraga burseriana

It cannot be bettered in beauty, is easy to please and eager to flower, is worth looking at in any season and long-lived: little wonder that *S. burseriana* has been a favourite for as long as kabschias have been admired. It is a native of the eastern Alpine chain, always on limestone or

34. One of the finest Kabschia species – *Saxifraga burseriana*.

dolomite formations and although it will inhabit rock fissures, its much commoner dwelling place is in the gravelly detritus below cliffs and escarpments where it seeks some shade from the worst heat of the day.

There are marked regional differences in the species, and the forms most often seen in cultivation have the character of those from the low-level, southern habitats of Italy and Austria. These make sturdy cushions of spiny, blue-grey leaves and have huge, long-stalked flowers, very early in the year.

To the north and east of Austria the plants have greener, dwarfer cushions and bloom later on shorter stalks. All have pure white, saucer-shaped flowers enhanced by golden stamens at their centres and their petal rims may be gently waved or finely scalloped. Flower stems vary in colour from pale green through sulphur to wine-red.

The early-flowering forms are really best grown as pot plants, to be brought under glass for their display. This protects their blooms from the ravages of winter weather and also allows the grower sheltered enjoyment of them. The dwarfer, later-flowering types are quite suited to the open garden, especially in troughs and tufa blocks. Many nurseries stock named clones of this species, such as S. 'Gloria', S. 'Brookside' and S. 'Snowdon', but these are the early types; the most compact, later forms are less easily obtained and may have to be raised from wild seed or cuttings from a selected plant.

Saxifraga caesia

This tough little sun-lover is widespread in Europe's mountains, always on calcareous rock, either in crevices or on very stony ground. Its cushion is hard and slow-growing with a hint of blue in its tiny grey leaves (*caesia* = bluish). The dainty cupped flowers are a cool white and held in small, open groups on slender stems to form a jostling crowd above the plant. Judged by its natural choice of places to

35. A resident of the Pirin Mountains – *Saxifraga ferdinandi-coburgii*. (A. M. Edwards)

live it should be drought-resistant, being frequently found in exposed locations where moisture appears to be scarce. As a garden plant it does have a measure of resistance to dry spells, but within limits; it will not brook the parching that sedums or some of the campanulas can withstand. *S. caesia* is happiest when given a well-drained slot between stones or in a scree, where it can root deeply. It can never be regarded as an easy plant in cultivation due to its unpredictable reactions; it may flourish in just one spot and refuse all others in the same garden. As an inmate of the alpine house it becomes more difficult to please and prone to dying off in patches.

In addition to having great charm as one of the miniatures of the Kabschia clan, *S. caesia* has further value in that it waits unusually long before coming into bloom, as late as the end of May or even early June, when other kabschias are long gone. So little is the variation in the species that there are no special or selected forms; no nursery offers a 'Gran-diflora' or a 'Superba'. Although plants can be raised from cuttings these perform less well than those grown from seed.

Saxifraga ferdinandi-coburgi

A Bulgarian saxifrage named after a king of that country, and not unsuitably, as this Kabschia does have a golden crown – of flowers. These are a solid, buttercup-yellow and are set in plenty at the height of spring, remaining at their best for two weeks or more. They are held in cymes of up to 12 on substantial stems above a close, grey-green cushion. The territory of the species is small, and confined to the Pirin and Rhodope mountains, with just one other occurrence in the north-eastern tip of Greece. Limestone clefts are its commonest haunts, though it does venture on to stony slopes at times, anywhere between the 1000 and 3000 metre contours.

In the climate of north-westEngland this is a saxifrage for growing in the open garden with confidence. It is totally hardy and reliable, will take the sun all day, is

rarely afflicted by pests or diseases and if battered by rain quickly recovers unscathed. Plant it in a rich scree or a well-prepared trough and it will settle there for years, never losing its willingness to flower. A cautionary footnote to all this praise concerns, yet again, the need to avoid poor forms, as there are some which flower sparingly (to say the least). If plants are acquired from a reputable nursery owning a good stock of Kabschias, then the form offered is likely to be a good one.

Saxifraga georgei

One of the most choice and successful of the saxifrages introduced from the Himalayas in recent years, making a fresh green, low dome of tiny crowded leaves. In early spring the beautifully-formed, almost stemless flowers group themselves over the surface of the cushion, their slightly translucent white petals distinctly separate and rising from a yellow ovary ringed with bright orange anthers. Although this little charmer never climbs very high in the great peaks it has pretty well spanned the Himalayan chain with its distribution, which starts in Nepal and stretches eastwards all the way to Tibet and China. Its usual haunts are moist, cool cliffs of granite or schist at altitudes approaching 3000 m (10000 ft).

Given excellent drainage and a gritty, open soil, or if grown in a block of tufa, *S. georgei* will endure the winter unaided, but pot-grown specimens are curiously less stoic and fare much better under glass. A torrid place will tax this plant beyond its limits, so choose an aspect which enjoys good light without being sun-struck in the summer months. The Himalayan saxifrages are distressed by low moisture levels at the root much more than their European counterparts, both whilst active and during their resting periods. The British summer, at its worst, is never too wet for them and in winter those under glass quickly become stressed, with fatal consequences, if the root-run is anything less than moist.

So minuscule and brittle are the leaf-

rosettes that taking cuttings is a task akin to micro-surgery and it is less exacting, though not easy, to collect and sow the seed. Growers lacking the essential keen eyesight, steady hand or patience will be pleased to find that several nurseries now list this saxifrage.

Saxifraga lilacina

More than ninety years ago this very special saxifrage was discovered in the eastern Himalayas and brought into cultivation. Since then all attempts to find it again have failed and every one of the thousands growing now and in the past come from that first introduction. Judging from early photographs and descriptions it has lost none of its original form and beauty, despite countless propagations by cuttings, which runs contrary to the belief that such repetition induces weakness and loss of quality. The flower colour is unique amongst the known kabschias: a strong violet on opening, then paling to lilac pink. This hue is evident in many of the early cultivated hybrids such as 'Jenkinsae', 'Irvingii' and 'Winifred', all of which had S. lilacina as a parent.

Little is known of the wild habitat, but it has been found that limy soils are not to its liking, nor is too much exposure to strong sunlight. Excessive shade, however, is detrimental to both the quantity and the colour of the flowers and so a place enjoying morning sunshine has the required balance. Given this and a well-drained compost the plant will slowly expand its dark-green cushion and cover it with a close-fitting cap of bloom every March or early April. Being Himalayan its need for generous watering, or rainfall, during the growing season should never be neglected and even in the depths of winter the roots must never encounter

36. A very mature and healthy plant of
     Saxifraga lilacina.

dryness. When grown in the alpine house the plant can suffer from mould attacks from autumn to early spring; these are rarely fatal if removal of the afflicted patches is prompt, but the plant is left mutilated and poor in flower. Specimens in troughs or beds with just a pane of glass for winter cover suffer much less from this blight, probably due to the vastly improved air circulation and the reliability of moisture at the root.

Saxifraga marginata

This easy-going and free-flowering species is found in many areas to the south and east of the Alps, from the spine of Italy to the hills of Yugoslavia and Greece. In each region it seems to have evolved somewhat separately, giving us a wealth of variants with quite distinctive characteristics. The Italians are the favourites, with their abundant, large flowers borne in cymes on sturdy stems, but all the forms are worth growing and a few, carefully chosen, will give a succession of blooms over several weeks, as their flowering times also differ. The one constant feature is the flower colour: the petals are a milky white and centre on a bright yellow bunch of stamens, giving the floral array a clean, fresh appeal.

Any free-draining, gritty soil will satisfy this kabschia and in many gardens even day-long exposure to the sun has no ill effects. It blooms early in the year, around mid-March, and heavy rain or sleet can mar the petals a little, but otherwise the plant is tough enough to take the seasons as they come. Contented specimens can live for a very long time and twenty years is not unusual. The low, spreading cushion is always attractive with its squat, slightly columnar leaf-rosettes of silvery grey and translucent edging to each leaf (hence *marginata*). Named forms are widely available from alpine nurseries and increase by cuttings or seed involves nothing out of the ordinary. A search around established plants will sometimes reveal self-sown off-spring which, although likely to be hybrids if there are other kabschias nearby, are nearly always handsome and interesting to grow on just to see what develops.

Saxifraga poluniniana

The third and final Himalayan, selected because of its excellent temperament, rapid growth and prolific flowering. It forms a very low, slightly lax cushion of small, succulent-looking leaves which it smothers with short-stemmed flowers of great charm. The emerging petals are pink, but quickly pale to a warm white as the flower opens fully, then the pink blush returns as the blooms age. This delightful behaviour is somewhat variable from plant to plant. The display is rather short-lived, being more or less over in a week, but for those few days it is superb. The choice and delicate appearance of the plant belies its strong constitution, for in all save the most severe winters it survives in the open garden without protection and blooms just as freely as it does in the alpine house or frame. Lengthy, wet periods in winter can cause some rotting of the cushion, yet such is its vigour that the blemishes are soon overgrown and by late spring have disappeared.

S. poluniniana was found in the region South of Anapurna, growing on moist cliffs in some shade, at altitudes around 3000 m (10000 ft). In cultivation it will accept full exposure to the sun if the moisture supply to the roots does not falter and seems to have no aversion to lime. The seed set by garden plants may well not come true; indeed this saxifrage has been used extensively of late to produce some of the exquisite hybrids recently raised. As cuttings are easy to root, however, there are no problems to increasing selected forms of this first rate

species. In captivity the flowers can be open in March and plants under glass have the advantage of protection for their flowers from the spoiling effects of heavy rain or severe frost.

Saxifraga scardica

From the almost moss-like cushions of S. georgei and other dwarfed species S. scardica takes us to the other extreme of Kabschia character. Its cushion is robust, with the individual leaf-rosettes clearly defined; the large, sharp-tipped leaves give the whole growth a stiff, prickly appearance. The flower stalks are similarly rigid and hold clusters of flowers well above the leafage. The form that is predominant in cultivation has pure white blooms, although there are colour variants in nature and it is surprising that growers have not striven harder to have them, for they are reported to range from pale pink to cerise. Mount Olympus is the best known location, but the specific name is derived from a less publicized occurrence on the Scardus range in Jugoslavia. Limestone rocks and screes are the typical habitats, usually at lower elevations around 2000 m (6500 ft) and in these the plants seek shade, but on Olympus they climb to almost 3000 m (10000 ft) where, at those cooler heights, they are able to occupy more exposed sites.

Whether by accident or misunderstanding this Kabschia has an undeserved reputation for difficulty in cultivation, perhaps because it has been assumed that a plant of such a tough and spiky nature would revel in sun and have reserves to combat drought. This might indeed be true of the high altitude forms, but for the remainder there is a need for shade in the midday hours and an avoidance of parching in the root-run. With some precautions made good, S. scardica is no trickier than many other kabschias. Specialist nurseries usually have a few plants in stock, but why not try some wild seed, with the possibility of raising a few of those elusive colour forms?

The 'Silvers'

Of all the genera and species which are defined as 'rock plants' few deserve that title more than the 'silver' saxifrages. The great majority of them require very little of the gardener's time or care for their well-being and give of their best year after year. Only a few of the species form true cushions, but there are some fine hybrids with the same habit. The flowers of many can be truly described as spectacular, arching far out from the plant in plumes and sprays and at a time when the spring flush of bloom in the rock garden is waning. The foliage makes symmetrical arrays of grey leaves embellished by lime encrustations, giving effects like frosted pewter, which is why they are called the 'silver' saxifrages. Look for them on the warm limestones of gorges and escarpments in the Maritime Alps, in the canyons of the Pyrenees or the cliffs above the Italian lakes, in sun and in shade, on the most inhospitable ground. Assume (rightly) that they can tolerate drought and know nothing other than perfect drainage at their roots. Bear these things in mind when creating places in the garden for the 'silvers' and they will give many seasons of pleasure in return.

37. The cliff residence of *Saxifraga callosa*.

Saxifraga callosa

So varied is this saxifrage that it can be difficult to believe that all the forms are of the one species. On some plants the leaves will not exceed three or four centimetres in length, yet their neighbours on the same mountain flank may sport them as thin straps up to 10 cm (4 in) long. Not all of the forms make a cushion of their leaf-rosettes, especially the lanky types, and 'clumps' would better describe them, but those with short leaves can build up quite a solid, even mound sufficient to qualify them for inclusion here. The lime-secreting pores are very conspicuous on the leaf margins, as though they had been carefully beaded with white paint. Several hundred flowers can be borne on a single stem, crowded in a rather one-sided panicle of up to 60 cm (2 ft) long, which is bowed down under the weight of bloom. the petals are a cool white and vary in width from plant to plant, the better varieties being those with the broadest petals.

The natural distribution of the species has a strange discontinuity. It occurs very locally at the far eastern end of the Pyrenees and then there is a large gap before it reappears in the Maritime Alps to spread eastwards and southwards into Italy, Sicily and Sardinia. The highest locations are at 2500 m (8000 ft), but generally they lie between 1000 and 2000 m (3600–6500 ft) and all are confined to limestones.

For the very best effect *S. callosa* should be planted in or on top of a wall or rock face, where its plumes will be unhindered and can form a cascade of flower. There are always young, non-flowering rosettes to be found in adult plants, often with a few roots already developed, making propagation an easy matter.

Saxifraga cochlearis

Although the cliffs on which this saxifrage grows can be sunlit for a portion of the day they are, for most of the time, shaded, yet in British gardens the plant shows no resentment of a fully exposed position.

The explanation for this may well lie in the availability of water, for whereas the garden-dweller is unlikely to be left to parch in dry weather, the wild plant must rely on reserves within the rock, and these are least where the sun strikes hardest and longest. Sunshine is certainly a feature of the two small regions to which *S. cochlearis* is endemic, in the foothills of the S.W. Alps, close to the Côte d'Azur. In bloom this species does not have the abundance of *S. callosa*, but is more delicate, with slender open panicles of fewer flowers, their whiteness emphasized, in the choicest forms, by the mahogany-red of the stems and branches. There is an almost crystalline look to the foliage caused by numerous lime-capped pores on the leaf surfaces. The slightly irregularly-splayed rosettes intermesh to form a shapely, rounded cushion which 'moulds' itself to the surface beneath it. References conflict on the meaning of the epithet *cochlearis*; some say 'shell-like' and others 'spoon-like', in reference to the leaf shape. There is a fair resemblance to a spoon, but little to suggest a shell.

The cultivation of this elegant 'silver' could hardly be easier. Any place that has been prepared for growing scree or crevice plants will suffice, whether in full sun or some shade. The species has few enemies; a slug or snail may occasionally nibble at a leaf or a few aphids might be found on a flower stem from time to time, but their effect is rarely serious. Nurseries often list two types of *S. cochlearis*, suffixed 'major' and 'minor', but it is strongly suspected that there are no real botanical differences involved; they are simply big 'uns and little 'uns selected from within the natural variation of the species. Single leaf-rosettes, taken as cuttings, can root within two or three weeks to make good-sized youngsters by the end of the season.

38.   The plumes of *Saxifraga cochlearis*.

How many plants offer us so much for so little?

Saxifraga paniculata

One of the commonest of the saxifrage species, encountered in many parts of the Northern Hemisphere and, not surprisingly, quite variable. Named forms abound, but one in particular has all the genuine character and quality of a cushion. Known in horticulture for years as either *S. baldensis* or *S. minutifolia*, it is now more accurately christened as *S. paniculata* var. *minutifolia*. It is by far the smallest of all the variants and occurs as a naturally diminutive form in the mountains by Lake Garda. The cushion is a compact mass of miniaturized leaf-rosettes and might be mistaken at first glance for one of the dwarfer kabschias. Whippy, reddish stems carry the yellow-eyed, white flowers in short panicles above the cushion.

There have never been any real difficulties to the growing of *S. paniculata* in any of its forms: it enjoys sunshine, is at home on poor, gritty soils or scree, and generally prefers life in the open garden to that in a pot. Once established, its life expectancy seems to be indefinite; it just carries on growing, needing very little in the way of care and attention. This saxifrage is predominantly a plant of non-calcareous formations, but limestone-dwelling types do exist, and included in these is *S.p.* var. *minutifolia*. Life on bare rocks and stony spoil had induced in *S. paniculata* a good resistance to drought; it is unperturbed by our hottest summers, nor do our wet winters cause it any apparent harm.

Every nursery seems to have its own favourite form of this species, and some still give it the label of *S. aizoon*. There is a variant with pinkish flowers (of wild origin) which will be found under the name of *S. paniculata rosea*.

Saxifraga valdensis

Last, and very much least, is this pigmy of the 'silvers'. So hoary and cramped are its stubby-leaved, heavily-encrusted rosettes, that seen in its wild habitat the plant resembles some small, warty-skinned creature huddled in the rock. It grows slowly and doggedly, in the crevices of limestone, schist and granite cliffs, seeming to favour the most exposed sites, indifferent to whether these are in sun or shade. As might be expected of a species which treats hardship as a way of life, it has an inherent resistance to drought and frosts. With these attributes, and being a member of an easily grown group of saxifrages, it might be assumed to have few problems for the grower, yet this is not so. The plant is a rarity in rock gardening, and seldom seen at exhibitions or shows. The probable cause of this is its vulnerability to attack by botrytis mould, particularly in winter. The safest approach to its cultivation is to treat it as a subject for the alpine house or covered plunge bed; and to maintain the characteristic compactness, together with good flowering, the compost used should be lean and sharply drained, and the light level must be high.

Those fortunate enough or skilled enough to initially satisfy *S. valdensis* will need patience; the cushion may double in size in three or four years and it will probably flower after settling down. It blooms modestly and in proportion to its stature, with a few dwarf cymes of white flowers in late May or June.

Only a single letter separates *S. valdensis* from *S. baldensis* (the erroneous synonym of *S. paniculata* var. *minutiflora*) and these continue to be confused, with the result that dwarf forms of *S. paniculata* are still to be found as counterfeits of the real thing, as also are diminutive clones of *S. cochlearis*. If in doubt refer to accurate descriptions in specialist publications such as those recommended later in this book.

S. valdensis is a plant to be grown in a special place where it has to be visited, admired and touched, to get the full enjoyment of its character and charm. A connoisseurs' item perhaps, but worth searching for and trying.

Footnote: Encrustation

In the introduction to the 'silvers' the limy encrustation of their leaves was recognized as a principal feature, but not explained, and as it is so curious it deserves a few more words.

The 'limy' deposit referred to in the text is calcium carbonate (of which tufa is formed) and is left behind as a crusty residue when beads of moisture, with calcium dissolved in them, are evaporated. These droplets are secreted by glands on the leaf surface, called hydathodes, and on humid days can be seen coating the leaves like dew. The benefit to the plant of the encrustation is not fully understood, though it must help to reduce moisture loss by reflection and insulation. Plants under glass build up heavier deposits than those outdoors, yet these still retain significant amounts despite the washing effect of rain.

The 'Mossies'

In truth 'moss' has many forms, but the word tends to evoke feathery foliage and soft, rounded growth, which fairly describes a typical cushion of the 'mossy'

saxifrages. The currently correct botanical classification for this branch of the family is: Section *saxifraga*, subsection *tripliner-vium* – which provides a good excuse for staying with the colloquial name! Just as mosses are to be found in a variety of habitats, from cool, shaded places to exposed rocks, so it is with these sax-ifrages. There are numerous species in the section, but many have little to entice the rock gardener, particularly in their floral displays, yet leaving aside the rank and the weedy there are some of refinement and quality which will grace the best collec-tion of cushion plants. It is from these that just a few have been selected to represent the best of the mossies. Their individual needs do differ slightly, but those chosen have a common dislike of parching, whether by excess sun or harsh, drying winds. Protecting them with shade and shelter must not, however, rob them of too much light, otherwise they become drawn and thinly flowered.

As cultivated plants they lie somewhere between the kabschias and the 'silvers' in the amount of care required to keep them satisfied. They need rather more mois-ture-retentive material in the soil mixture than the other two types as they suffer earlier from drought; a 20% addition of peat or leafmould is adequate. Aphid infestation can be quite advanced before it is visibly apparent, by which time the damage wrought may be considerable. A close look into the centre of one or two leaf-rosettes at regular intervals serves as an early warning system. Apart from these simple attentions the 'mossies' have few vices and can be grown as pot, trough or bed subjects with little trouble and much enjoyment.

Saxifraga cebennensis

In the huge limestone plateau of the French Cevennes, streams and torrents active over millennia have cut numerous gorges deep into the rock and on the sheer, shaded walls of these grows *S. cebennensis*. It builds a fairly large, hemi-spherical cushion of soft, rather sticky leaves and envelops it each spring with an orderly mass of crisp, white flowers, set in twos and threes on short, pliant stalks. The springiness of the compact foliage serves to protect the cushion from the light blows of falling pebbles, but more serious impacts by dislodged stones (or perhaps a careless tug from the weeding gardener) can tear out a tuft. Such wounds trigger another form of resilience in the plant whereby it produces new rosettes to heal the cavity and restore its even surface.

The symmetry and texture of its cushion and its copious flowering have made this species very popular with those who exhibit alpine plants, and as a result it is more often seen in a pot than in a garden. A false impression is thus created of a plant needing the skill and facilities of the expert grower, whereas in reality it is quite tough and able to fend for itself 'out-doors' with the other residents of the rock garden. A cool but not sunless nook will suffice, in the rockwork, trough or raised bed, provided that the roots can always find moisture yet have a perfectly drained run. Slugs and snails pass it by if there are more toothsome leaves in the vicinity. Plants are easily come by in nurseries and single leaf-rosettes usually root without fuss in a simple propagator.

Saxifraga exarata

No sheltered chasm for this mountain-dweller; it inhabits the cliffs, boulders and stony slopes of the sub-alpine and alpine levels. The distribution must be one of the most extensive in the genus, starting at the northern end of Spain and following the mountains of central Europe, then to the Carpathians, the Balkan peninusla, Greece and yet further east to north-western Iran. As might be expected, this great spread of locations has brought considerable variation to the species and presently there are five recognized sub-species. Natural hybridization has added to the complexity of identification: there are at least eleven reported from various sites. Some of the sub-species are endemic to particular rock types, but others are equally at home on limestone, basalt, schists or granite. As the reader will appreciate, it is impossible to describe a 'typical' *S. exarata*; the best that can be said is that the cushion is generally low and compact and that the flowers are plentiful, ranging in colour from white, through cream and yellow to (rarely) a dusky red.

There are no significant problems in the cultivation of this multifarious plant and it needs no artificial aids for garden life. Understandably it is regularly confused with *S. pubescens* by sellers and buyers alike and it is worth noting that *S. moschata*, formerly a separate species, has now been absorbed into *exarata*. Definitely a plant to be seen, and seen in flower, before acquiring.

Saxifraga pedemontana

Regarded until very recently as a less than garden-worthy plant, but then came the introduction of a form from a newly-discovered location on Mt Kasbek in the Caucasus, which stole the show when exhibited. The fairly large leaf-rosettes of this newcomer are a light green and packed tightly to form an attractively-shaped cushion. The flowers are also larger than is usual in the section, and can cap the entire cushion in a well-grown specimen. There is an iciness to the white of the flowers and this, together with the pearly sheen of the petals and the pale acid-yellow of the stamens, imparts an extraordinary cool and elegant beauty to the display.

Contrary to early cultivation reports *S. pedemontana* will survive the winter without glasshouse or frame protection, but responds with only a fraction of its flowering potential. Wherever it is grown it will appreciate light shading in the summer months. There are no extra ingredients required in the soil mixture, but as the wild habitats are only on acidic formations, calcareous soils and grits are

39. *Saxifraga pedemontana* has a pearly cast to its elegant flowers.

best avoided. There is little doubt that alpine house specimens are much superior in the quality and wealth of bloom, but of course, with that confinement come the problems of botrytis and red spider mite; nevertheless the reward of a superbly flowered plant justifies the battle against these foes.

Saxifraga pubescens

In contrast to the two foregoing species *S. pubescens* is extremely localized, being found only in the eastern ranges of the Pyrenees; even so, it has enough variation to warrant a division into two sub-species: ssp. *pubescens* and ssp. *iratiana*. The latter is the high alpine form, living generally

40. An infant *Saxifraga pubescens*, already showing its 'flower power'.

41. *Saxifraga pubescens* in its natural haunt. (R. Rolfe)

42. The rather loose cushion of *Saxifraga* × *patens* blooms heartily.

43. A very modern saxifrage hybrid – 'Peter Burrow'. (R. Rolfe)
44. *Saxifraga* 'Golden Prague' is as colourful in seed as it is in flower.

above 2500 m (8000 ft) on exposed acid schists and is, in appearance, a refined version of ssp. *pubescens*, with tighter, neater growth and richer flowering. Neither sub-species has a constitution suited to the hurly burly of the open garden; they are for pot culture and need protection plus attention to survive. When grown as an alpine house or plunge bed plant it requires a free-draining but not too lean soil mixture (typically a half-and-half blend of J.I. No. 2 and grit), plenty of fresh air and shade from the hottest sun. Aphids can invade the foliage at any time of year and botrytis can spread rapidly through the crowded rosettes in late autumn and winter.

The availability of ssp. *iratiana* is quite good, but look for plants with the added attractiveness of fine, crimson veining in their white petals. The other sub-species is far harder to find, mainly because it is much less popular with its laxer growth and scantier bloom.

The Hybrids
Kabschia types:
Dozens of articles and almost an entire book* have been devoted to these hybrids. There are hundreds of them and more are

being contrived all the time. The few examples offered here have been selected to represent the scope of form and colour that exists. A great deal of work has been done of late to rationalize and discipline the naming of hybrids, yet there are still pockets of resistance and indifference remaining where the old names cling on, to the confusion of those who seek the 'true plant'. The names used in the following adhere to the new code, as do the labels of good, responsible nurseries.

The yellows are typified by the old but ever-popular S. 'Faldonside' and the newer S. 'Valerie Finnis', both of which have a grey-green cushion of crowded, sharp leaves. The flowers of 'Faldonside' are large, set on short stalks and are the colour of a ripe lemon, whereas those of 'Valerie Finnis' are a little smaller, paler and almost sessile, with a slightly metallic sheen to the petals. A warmer tone is set by S. 'Galaxie', which flowers very early (January–February) in a deeper shade and is tinged with orange near the stamens. Its cushion is slow-growing, dense and has small leaf-rosettes.

The whites of the wild species are so pure and plentiful that it is no surprise to find that there are fewer white than coloured hybrids, but one which cannot go unmentioned is the cross between *S. tombeanensis* and *S. marginata* named S. 'Vahlii'. Its large snow-white flowers are several to a stem and combine to hide totally the strong, hard cushion for a full two weeks of April.

The pinks vary from a gentle blush to a rosy glow and are seen nowhere better than in S. 'Johana Kellerer', which makes a vigorous, full cushion bearing quite long stems, each with flowers of a rich pink; S. 'Josef Capek', has large, full-petalled flowers of palest salmon-pink and a rosy

45. One of the many Kabschia hybrids (*Saxifraga* 'Galaxie').

46. Plants race to produce flowers in the brief mountain spring.

tint to their margins, sitting almost stemless on a dense blue-green cushion. From the very latest generation of hybrids, in which the small Himalayan kabschias have been crossed with the very old favourite S. 'Winifred', have come new pinks such as S. 'Red Poll' and S. 'Peter Burrow', both having masses of rosy, petite flowers smothering their quick-growing, low cushions.

There are many, many more and it is really a matter for the grower to see them in flower and to check their individual cultural requirements before deciding upon which to try, as some are only suitable for cultivation under glass whilst others are quite at ease in the open.

*Porophyllum Saxifrages, Horny, Webr and Byam-Grounds.

47. A 'silver' saxifrage hybrid (*S. cochlearis* × *S. callosa*).

'Silver' *types*

Bona fide cushions are rare in the crosses of 'encrusted' species, the prevalent forms being mats and clumps. Examples of those which do qualify are: *S.* × *burnattii*, a naturally occurring hybrid of *S. paniculata* and *S. cochlearis*, the latter giving the plant its close, domed growth. The white flowers are of good form and held in panicles on long, red-tinted stems. The very slow-growing *S.* 'Cecil Davies' must be one of, if not *the* most beautifully patterned of the 'silvers': the lime beading is exact and prominent on the shapely leaves. Its flowers are produced sparingly and are very similar to those of *S.* × *burnattii*. The zest for living makes *S.* 'Whitehill' one of the most dependable and enjoyable hybrids; it is weatherproof, not fussy about soil or siting and rarely troubled by pests or diseases. The leaf-rosettes, with eye-catching encrustation, are stained claret at their centres and pile together in a low impregnable mound, from which sprays of white bloom rise in profusion.

'Mossy' *types*

Most of the 'mossy' hybrids have such vigour that they are much too invasive for any patch where true alpine plants are cultivated; the robust pillows and bolsters that they form are safer as edgings to drives and pathways or carpet plants beneath open, taller-growing plants. Dwarf forms are few, but *S.* 'Cloth of Gold' makes a striking tuffet of yellow and puts up paper-white flowers on slim stalks; a good 'nurseryman's plant' that attracts buyers like moths to a flame and then usually lives but a short time before creating a vacancy for a replacement! 'Sunstroke' is the usual post mortem. The helpfully-named *S.* 'Pixie' has an attractive 'dumpling' of a cushion with pink, cupped flowers on short stems and is, unusually, at its best in full light. Another from the fairy world is *S.* 'Elf', a true miniature in its growth, but it raises lengthy stalks to carry its carmine flowers. The most vibrant colour is that of *S.* 'Peter Pan' with crimson flowers and a compact cushion.

CHAPTER 3

The cushion plant 'oddfellows'

'Oddfellows' was chosen as a heading for this chapter not because its plants are any less attractive or desirable, but to separate them as being of genera which have too few species in cultivation to be grouped. The low numbers may be due to: (a) there being only one or two cushion types in an otherwise wholly 'conventional' genus; (b) a lack of access to the wild plants; (c) there being very few species in the genus; or (d) the lack of success in cultivating them or the fact that they are not worth growing.

48. Acantholimons revel in hot, stony ground. (R. Rolfe)

Acantholimon

Pride of place usually goes to *A. venustum*, a humped mass of needle-pointed grey-green leaves which can attain the size and shape of half a football in just a few years. Its flowers, of clear rose pink, are carried

on arching stems in early summer. Many references describe this species as needing alpine house treatment, yet in a friend's North Yorkshire garden several fine specimens survive all weathers and bloom unfailingly. The sunny limestone scree is perhaps the best place for this spiky rival to the cacti, although any well drained, sandy soil might suffice. The only other species that is firmly established in cultivation is *A. glumaceum*, but it tends to sprawl and stray from the cushion form. Both are native to the mountains that link Afghanistan to the Black Sea and favour rocks and debris at high altitudes.

There are other choice species, mostly smaller and compact, such as: *creticum*, from Crete, *A. hohenackeri*, from the eastern Caucasus and *A. libanoticum* from the Lebanon, but they are scarcely in cultivation and little is known about growing them. It would be prudent for those lucky enough to obtain any of these to treat them, initially, as alpine house subjects, giving them a gritty, open compost and plenty of light. Regular watering through spring and summer and a just moist state whilst at rest should be in order. Propagation is difficult: it is unknown for these plants to set seed in the UK and the chances of rooting cuttings are small. Seed from wild sources offers the most hope.

Arabis androsacea

Without first-hand acquaintance with this plant in its native habitat it is difficult to be informative about its lifestyle, particularly as reference material is terse and repetitive. The impression gained from the descriptions offered by several authors is that they have all resorted to the brief notes of Reginald Farrer in his great work, *The English Rock Garden*. There are five exact repeats of the rather vague location 'Turkish Armenia' and none provides any detail at all regarding – for example – the terrain, the exposure, the nature of earth

or rock in which the plant lives. Judged by the silky hairiness of the small, tight cushions seen in cultivation, this species has evolved protection against the moisture-robbing effects of sun and drying winds, and the extensive rooting behaviour suggests that screes or fissures are where it will be found. In captivity the plant is slow-growing, and the absence of specimens much over 10 cm (4 in) diameter reveals the limit to adult life. As there is no mention on record of large cushions in the wild, it is possible that this growth rate and lifespan are comparable to those in nature.

One or two rock gardening publications imply that *A. androsacea* is suitable for open garden culture, yet it takes skill and attention to achieve a sound and unblemished specimen, even with overhead protection. If it is treated and cared for in the same way as the cushion androsaces it will slowly and compactly build a little rounded hummock of silvered leaf-rosettes and provide plenty of its white flowers on short scapes.

There is a fairly consistent stock of this arabis in at least two of the leading alpine plant nurseries, and garden-gathered seed is often listed, but whether these are still true is doubted by some pundits. To avoid their scepticism and be reasonably certain of growing the real thing it is best to raise stock from wild seed (collected by authorized agents).

Asyneuma pulvinatum

On the sheer faces of limestone cliffs, high in the Anatolian mountains of western Turkey, *A. pulvinatum* fights against extinction, seeking faults and crevices in the hard rock as refuges from competition. It is regarded as a relict species, and botanists are still unsure as to whether it is truly an asyneuma or something close, but of greater antiquity. The plant's narrowly elliptic leaves are in fairly open rosettes, but so closely arranged as to give the cushion a very smooth profile. In high summer the miniature harebell flowers rise on very short scapes, just above the leaves, delicately coloured in blue or lilac. This is a plant of merit and quality, deserving more attention than it presently receives, but its late July flowering causes it to miss the season of alpine plant shows, and in consequence few rock gardeners are aware of its beauty and character.

Not surprisingly, the cultivated plant requires faultless drainage and very good light. Although there are scarcely any useful references to its culture, this species should be a prime candidate for growing in tufa under cover. When cultivated as a pot-dwelling specimen it is best kept in the alpine house, given a gritty compost, and treated in the same way as the difficult campanulas, such as *C. morettiana*. Autumn and winter bring the threat of fungal infections in the cushion, and to combat these the compost should be maintained in an only-just-moist condition. All possible measures must be taken to dispel humid, dank states under glass.

It is not easy, but possible, to propagate the plant from cuttings, and by this means the specialist nurseries are able to offer limited numbers on an occasional basis. Wild seed is hardly ever available, and rightly so if we are to help in the survival of the remaining colonies.

Bolax gummifera

Although introduced from South America by Ruth Tweedie some thirty years ago, *B. gummifera* has been strangely neglected and has remained a rarity in cultivation. Neither the Alpine Garden Society nor the Scottish Rock Garden Club have given it any attention in their publications, yet when it makes one of its all too brief appearances on the show bench it draws considerable interest and admiration. True, the cushion is never smothered in bloom, but this is a plant with a particularly fine foliage effect. The grey-green concentric leaves of its quite large rosettes splay into three finger-like lobes with a slight thickening and bleaching to their edges, emphasizing their outlines like a rime of frost. The cushion is soft, with an evenly-rounded profile and the whole appearance is one of pleasing, delicate geometry. In cultivation the plant will occasionally produce the behaviour which gave it its name, exuding a gummy substance from between its rosettes. We are ignorant of why it does this. Cultivated plants can be long-lived and of considerable size; specimens in pots have been exhibited with unblemished, hemispherical cushions of 30 cm (12 in) diameter.

An open, gritty soil mixture, enriched with humus, will keep the plant content in a raised bed or trough open to full light. Winter cover is a wise precaution for any grown thus. A suitable potting compost is equal parts of J.I. No. 1, peat or leafmould, and grit. Despite its preference for peaty deposits in the wild, the plant has some tolerance of lime in cultivation and has been grown to good effect in tufa. Cuttings usually root well if taken when the leaf-rosettes show signs of dividing. Seed is rarely offered and nursery plants are hard to find.

Celmisia

Two species from this great genus in the southern half of the globe have an immediate attraction for the cushion grower. Both live in the mountains of New Zealand's South Island, on exposed flanks of frost-shattered stone, where there is good snow cover in winter and plentiful rain when the plants are busy with growth and flower.

Celmisia argentea constructs an impeccable cushion of closely ordered leaf-rosettes, their spiny leaves radiating evenly and rigidly, with an unusually bright, steely sheen during late spring and summer. Later in the year this shiny coating is dulled and the underlying green of the foliage sets the colour tone for the dormant period. The celmisias belong to the daisy-flowered members of the *Compositae* family, and this species can put up a fair display of sessile, slightly untidy white blooms with pointed 'petals'.

There are claims that the plant can be grown in tufa, which is surprising as there is no mention of calcareous rock in references to the natural habitat.

Celmisia sessiliflora is always described, in its wild form, as creating a mat or patch (up to 1 metre across), but in cultivation it produces a neat hemisphere. Perhaps this is its juvenile form, which is never outgrown in captivity, or it may be that our inferior light levels draw the growth upwards. (It might even be a hybrid.) Whatever the cause, the plant which we have in cultivation is a striking and a worthy inclusion for a collection of cushions.

The leaf-rosettes are large and boldly structured; the long awl-shaped leaves have a pale, silver-grey coating and radiate stiffly to mimic an open sea anemone. Away from its natural home *C. sessiliflora* flowers irregularly and sparsely, with blooms resembling small, white dahlias, sunk among the mass of rosettes, in strict accordance with its specific name.

Some of the finest celmisias are grown in the gardens of Northern Ireland, where the 'soft' climate brings regular, refreshing rain and cooling winds from the Atlantic ocean, a firm indication of the celmisias' needs in cultivation. Neither of the above species requires any protection from the spring and summer weather, unless it be the supply of plentiful water in dry, hot spells. They are totally hardy, yet will benefit from an amount of coddling whilst at rest, as apparently they can discard much of their root system when shutting down for the winter, and reach a state which might prove vulnerable to the cold, wetness ahead. The beautiful specimens admired at the shows live outdoors from April to the end of October, but are then taken under glass for their hibernation.

Crassula sediformis

A very easy and totally weatherproof cushion that will grow almost anywhere in the rock garden and require the absolute minimum of attention. Unfortunately its origins and identity have no corresponding simplicity. It is one of the most frequently-seen plants in the alpines on sale at nurseries, garden centres and even high street shops, where it shows its toughness by surviving ill treatment, forgetful waterers and over-long residence in a small pot, but it does suffer from confu-

49. A superb example of the cushion grower's skill – *Diosphera asperuloides*, syn. *Trachelium asperuloides*. (E. Jarrett)

sion of name. The one used to head this description may or may not be correct; the identical plant will be found under *C. sedoides*, *C. sedifolia* and, curiously, *C.* 'Basutoland'. It gives of its best on lean, rapidly-drained and sunny ground, where it will form a domed mass of bright-green and somewhat fleshy leaf-rosettes, which resemble those of *Sedum spathulifolium* and others (as the name implies). If the summer provides some reasonably long periods of hot, sunny weather a few stocky flowering stems should rise a little clear of the cushion to bear the crowded umbels of small, white, starry flowers, each of which is enhanced by the wine-red ovary at its centre. Some of the blooms will produce fertile seed and this is transported, somehow, to other parts of the garden, giving rise to the subsequent appearance of young plants in surprising and unexpected places, but never in numbers that might prove to be a nuisance.

Left undisturbed and undamaged *C. sediformis*, if we can call it that, will continue to expand and becomes a shallow, creeping mound that defeats any weeds trying to invade the occupied area with its impregnable armour of packed rosettes.

Diosphaera asperuloides (syn. *Trachelium asperuloides*)

It is necessary to cheat just a little in order that this dainty and valuable plant can be included in the cushions, for although it grows in the approved manner, it does need a light 'haircut' after flowering to maintain compactness. Older catalogues and references put it in the genus *Trachelium*, but more recently there has been a reversion to *Diosphera*. Both are of the family *Campanulaceae* and originate in the limestones of Greece.

The foliage is a pale green and composed of reflexed tufts of strap-shaped, slightly glossy leaves, interlocking to form a smooth mound. It is not until July that the plant comes into bloom, with powder-blue, starry flowers in groups of up to five, held on short shoots above the cushion. The floral effect is delicate and delightful, occurring when the blooms of other cushions are long past. In the alpine house this is not a difficult plant to

grow, using a sharply-drained compost and avoiding over-shading, which will draw the growth out of character. Outdoors, even if well protected in the winter, its constitution is not adequate to withstand the regular wettings and harsher conditions, though this may not hold true for drier, kindlier climates. When the flowering cycle is over, most growers trim back the extended shoots and stems to restore the clean profile of the cushion.

Propagation is easily achieved by cuttings taken as ripe, unflowered shoots in July–August. Not a difficult plant to run to earth in the specialist nurseries. Slugs and aphids are the major foes and should be watched out for at all times.

Edraianthus pumilio (syn. Wahlenbergia pumilio)

Nothing could do better justice to this Dalmation mountain plant than an extract from the praises heaped upon it by Reginald Farrer, in which he describes it as 'the jewel of the family ... built of spiny, glistening, pointed little leaves, with their upper surfaces coated in silvery, close-piled silk, and their mass in early summer hidden from view beneath a dense settlement of great lilac-lavender cups, sitting close over the cushion and gazing sturdily up to the day'. A little over the top by modern literary standards perhaps, but giving a good portrait of a fine plant. Yet its merits do not end there. It is a willing and undemanding subject for the grower, content in a stony, gritty soil, in a sunny bed or trough and equally content when kept in a pot of lean compost. In nature it is a plant of limestone summits, finding all its needs in narrow crevices or shattered rock and able to flourish on the most exposed of crags.

The floral display comes at that time in the rock garden when the great spring flush has waned and new colour is so valuable, at the end of May and into June. *E. pumilio* has few enemies in the garden; the slugs and snails will chew it only as a last resort, and even the aphids only stray

50. **The floral abundance of *Edraianthus pumilio*, growing in the contrived crevice of a trough.**

51. Some of North America's eriogonums make fine cushions in the rock garden.

on to it now and then. In growth it is moderately paced, attaining a fist-sized tuffet in about four years. Cuttings are a good source of new plants and are usually taken in July from strong, unflowered shoots with all dead and dying leaves stripped away. In some years self-sown seedlings may appear around the plant, if it is growing in a trough or scree, and these are easily winkled out for potting up. Strangely, tufa-grown specimens do not thrive quite as well as might be expected, making rather scruffy cushions with bald patches developing when the plant is relatively young. These presumably indicate an insufficiency of some important nutrient. This undernourished look creeps into elderly plants and nothing will reverse it, so when it appears, usually after six or seven years, the plant should be replaced, after thanking it for the pleasure it has given.

Eriogonum shockleyi

In the mountains of Nevada in the USA, there are slopes which present an arid and inhospitable landscape, drenched in sun, hot and stony. The term 'raised desert' is used to describe the terrain; no place, it would seem, to look for choice rock plants, yet the baked earth supports a

highly evolved and varied flora, including this handsomely cushioned and closely-flowered species of *Eriogonum*. Its leaves have a succulent-like plumpness about them that suggests a capability to conserve and store moisture; they cluster in fairly open rosettes and have a silvered, felty appearance generated by a dense coating of fine hairs. The visual effect is heightened by a pinkish tinge that develops in old and declining foliage, glimpsed here and there in the array. In flower the plant is striking, with spherical heads of white, cream or pale yellow bloom raised just above the mound of the cushion by upright stems. As they age the flowers alter in colour to become infused with a gentle pink.

Even when given a permanent place in the alpine house this plant is not easy to satisfy nor to keep in character. Under our lower-strength and less frequent sunshine the growth tends to lose its compactness and flowers are fewer than in nature. If possible, cultivated specimens should be brought out from under glass whenever the summer sun is shining and returned at the first hint of rain. Winter watering should provide only enough to keep the life forces ticking over, and in the growing period must never err on the generous side. Cuttings can be rooted, if taken as healthy shoots about four weeks after the plant has completed its May/June flowering. If fresh seed can be obtained, a reasonable proportion ought to germinate, but it is the growing on that has given us the major difficulties. Very gritty compost provides the openness and freedom from over-moistness that the plant must have, but must be periodically enriched with a half-strength liquid feed to maintain an adequate level of nutrients. The latter applies only to summer watering.

Eritrichium nanum

Given the right situation E. nanum will make a respectable cushion, crowding its dark-green, hirsute leaves into a low mound, but it is the flowers that capture the wonder and delight of all who climb high in the European Alps: they are an intense blue, just hinting at turquoise and neatly spread rather than massed over the foliage. Each has a prominent centre of rich yellow, which turns to orange as the bloom matures. Until an ascent has reached the 2400 m (8000 ft) contour it is pointless to look for E. nanum, but above that level it is plentiful in a number of regions. The great majority of locations are on exposed rocky slopes of non-calcareous formations that have reliable winter snow cover. On these the plants may hug the ground, making small mats amongst the stones and tufts of grass, but in niches sheltered from the wind the cushion form prevails. So often are the colonies found only on acidic granites, basalts and conglomerates that the plant is frequently classified as a lime-hater, but search in the high limestone boulder fields of the Dolomites and there it will be discovered growing and flowering just as strongly and brilliantly, in the crannies of the great fallen blocks.

Almost since rock gardening began there have been countless attempts made to coax this high alpine into lowland captivity, but it will have none of it. Every few years there is a claim of success that is shown to be invalid when the specimen is put on display – a lax, tired-looking hump with a few insipid flowers, all the marvel lost. Enquiries about its progress, made in the following year, will almost always be met with a sad shake of the owner's head. Every imaginable method and treatment have been applied to E. nanum, but even in the best cases a year or two of promising progress ends in decline or sudden death. Perhaps someone will discover the key (if there is one) to keeping the plant alive and, more importantly, persuading it to flower with all the impact and vibrance it achieves so effortlessly in the mountains, but the sobering fact is that after a hundred years of trying we are still failing.

Gypsophila aretioides

Of all the cushions this has to be one of the hardest and most compacted. Its tiny, linear leaves are a rich bottle-green and splay in neat, flat rosettes, each interlocking with the next to create an almost smooth skin over the markedly domed growth. The immediate impression given by the plant is one of hard-won survival in hostile places, and such is true, for it lives in the mountains of Iran. The other location is high in the Caucasus on windswept rocks, where G. aretioides var. caucasica holds out against comparably unfriendly elements and has an almost identical appearance. Old and very large plants are collected, dried and used as fuel by the farmers and herders of those mountains.

Somewhat unexpectedly, the species and its variety are not overly difficult to grow in our quite different and kindlier garden environments. Both have been successfully established on sunny scree beds in the southern areas of England, and pot-

52. The golden fleece of *Haastia pulvinaris*.

grown specimens are a common sight on the show benches, holding true to their natural character and achieving great size and age. Not in character, however, is the meagreness of flower on cultivated plants; at best a few undersized versions of the pearly-white stars that ought to merge in plenty over the whole of the cushion.

Potting composts are generally of the half-and-half type, with no fuss needed in their preparation, but drainage must be immaculate. When grown in a tufa block or cliff the plant becomes even more tight and impenetrable, but is still not persuaded to bloom as it should. Seed is hardly ever available and propagation is reliant upon cuttings, which are rather slow to root and fiddlesome to handle. Periodically a specialist nursery will build up a small stock for sale.

Haastia pulvinaris

Small wonder that *H. pulvinaris* is a strange and remarkable plant, for it lives on arid, rocky slopes up to 2700 m (9000 ft), which in summer are alternately baked by strong sun and chilled by intensely cold, fog-laden winds. It must be the hairiest of all cushions, and has presumably developed this extremely hirsute state to combat the elements. After it has emerged from the thawing snow, under which it was snugly insulated by its self-made blanket, the countless hairs gather beads of water from the fogs and rain, to maintain the body of the plant in a permanently wet condition. Philipson and Hearn, in their very informative book *Rock Garden Plants of the Southern Alps* (New Zealand), tell us that: "... if you force your hand into the hummocks it is surprising to find them as wet as a sphagnum bog, even in mid-summer".

Within the woolly mound is a system of strong branches, much like candelabra, and heavily wrapped in old foliage, with the appearance and texture of kapok. At the tips of the shoots rising from the branches are the living leaves, totally hidden in the whorls of silky hair that sprout from them, evident only as a yellowy-green tint to the rosette centres, but the overall effect of the cushion surface is that of a lamb's fleece. One look at the plant is enough to convince many growers that it needs permanent protection, yet it can be grown outside, open to the weather from spring to autumn. If treated thus, the only harmful features of our British climate are hot, dry periods or

abnormally wet summers. Whilst at rest the plant does need to be sheltered against wettings, but it must never want for moisture at its roots.

In nature *H. pulvinaris* shares its inhospitable locations with certain of the cushion raoulias, and it will accept the same cultivation conditions as the raoulias. It would seem logical then to use a similar compost, but experience has shown that more drainage material is necessary. A blend that has proved suitable is made up of: 1 part J.I. No. 1, 1 part leafmould and 3 parts grit.

The flowering of the plant can pass unnoticed, being only visible as a tuft of pappus hairs at the centres of the rosettes. Seed is periodically available from New Zealand sources, and propagation from single shoot cuttings is often successful. Young plants are occasionally offered by nurseries.

Helichrysum pagophillum

An all-weather cushion for the garden, trough or pot, which looks difficult, but is in fact quite tolerant and adaptable. It is a native of the Drakensburg Mountains of south-east Africa, near Lesotho, and is found at heights around 3000 m (10000 ft), where it chooses moist, peaty soils overlying pulverized rock. There it makes irregular, humped patches that give little hint of the perfection in form that cultivated specimens can produce. The cushion is a tight, even mass of small-leaved, hairy rosettes with an overall light silver-grey appearance. The flowers are not a winsome feature, being a straw colour and almost a distraction to the handsomeness of the dome, but this is not a problem with plants in captivity, which bloom sparingly if at all.

Although of relatively recent introduction *H. pagophillum* has become reliably established in cultivation and is a regular entry in the foliage classes of alpine plant shows. As plants can be raised from cuttings quite readily, they are not hard to find on the stalls and in the catalogues of several nurseries. This is a fairly vigorous grower, typically attaining a diameter of some 25 cm (10 in) within three years of starting from a rooted cutting. There are several confirmed reports of its success as an unprotected garden plant, requiring only an open site in a peaty, well drained soil, and it has been grown as a trough subject without trouble. As a pot-grown plant it requires regular repotting to keep pace with its healthy and enthusiastic expansion. There are not many easily pleased yet well-behaved and structured cushions, but this is one, and a year-round asset to any rock garden.

Helichrysum sessiloides (syn. H. sessile)

The Drakensburg mountains of Natal, in South Africa, feature cliffs and screes of basalt, and in their crevices grow several fine alpines, including this admirable cushion plant. Contrary to what might be expected of a species from the mountain ranges of a hot country in the Southern Hemisphere, it has taken well to the British climate and become safely established in our collections, since its introduction in the 1970s. The plant has a determination to form an immaculate mound of its dark-green, silvery-haired leaf-rosettes, without any assistance from the grower, and is content with a gritty, neutral or slightly acid soil in a sunny, perfectly-drained spot. The peak of its attractiveness comes in spring, when the acorn-shaped, silver-white flower buds emerge from the foliage. Later, on sunny days, these open to display the yellow-centred 'everlasting' flowers, but the effect is not so pristine, and the grower waits for cloudy weather, when the flowers close and the charm is restored. The floral cycle lasts for many weeks, during which time

53. *Helichrysum sessiloides*, displaying its pearly flower buds on a raised scree bed.

the plant puts on new growth, and in this it is no slouch: five-year-old cushions can be at least 30 cm (12 in) across and still retain their good looks.

Where the winters are drier than in north-west England, overhead protection for the resting plant may not be needed, but it is a prudent insurance against disfigurement by lasting wetness. Single rosette cuttings, taken in June or July from the rim of the cushion, can be expected to form adequate roots in about five weeks, and by the end of the growing season will have a good development to see them through the winter. For pot-grown plants a half-and-half compost is quite satisfactory, but the growth rate should be accommodated by generous repotting, at least once per year. The more specialized alpine nurseries should list this obliging and valuable cushion plant.

Kelseya uniflora

Not a true cushion plant at all, more a compressed, stunted mass of tough little branches, twigs and leaves forming a cushion shape, but it must be included for its unique growth, its triumph over awesome conditions and the fact that it is held in high esteem by growers of cushion plants and fascinates all who see it. This is a shrub that has adapted to live on highly exposed limestone cliffs and rock slopes at around 3000 m (10000 ft), where the average annual rainfall is in the order of 30 cm (12 in) and occurs almost exclusively in spring and early winter. The prevailing weather pattern subjects the plants to cold, dry winter periods and hot, arid summers, adding to these strong, dehydrating winds that can blow at any time of the year. Assailed by this hostile climate *K. uniflora* seeks no shelter, but toughs it out on vertical faces and steep rockpiles, putting on no more (and often less) than a centimetre of growth in a year, and survives for many decades, stubbornly building its defiant cushion. The locations are all in the USA, in the Big Horn mountains of Wyoming and other ranges in Montana and Idaho.

The flowers are reminiscent of hawthorn blossom and can be white or tinted with pink, but they are tiny and held tight to the diminutive, grey-green leaves. In the wild and in cultivation the

54. An unusually fine specimen of the cliff-dwelling shrub *Kelseya uniflora*.

plant can make a brave attempt to cover itself with bloom. (It is of the same family as the rose!)

It is obvious from its lifestyle that *K. uniflora* will be intolerant of anything but perfect drainage and is unaccustomed to meeting soil in its root run; accordingly composts used are very open and lean. At the most generous the blend should contain no less than 50% grit or fine chippings. Crushed tufa can be used as an alternative drainage component, in which case it should form ⅔ of the mixture, the remainder being J.I. No. 1 or a blend of leafmould and fine loam. The best specimens in cultivation are invariably provided with flakes of stone or slate beneath their cushions to isolate the base from any moistness at the surface of the compost. Plants are grown successfully in open garden conditions, but tend to flower less well than those given alpine house treatment. The outdoor plants are often in tufa or a contrived crevice and usually positioned so that overhead protection can be fitted above the cushion for the wetter months. Pot-grown plants require regular supplies of water in spring and summer, but at other times the compost should be maintained in a just-moist state.

Seed is sometimes in the lists sent out by American rock gardening organizations, and occasionally nursery plants are to be had in this country. Cuttings of partially ripe shoots, taken in June or July, may be rooted in a simple propagator using sand. The use of rooting hormone can assist the process, but is not essential.

Myosotis

Of the twenty-five or so species of *Myosotis* that are native to the Southern Alps of New Zealand, almost all deserve a place in the rock garden, and two of them are thoroughbred cushion plants.

Myosotis pulvinaris has been very well described by Dr John Richards, in his account of a field trip to its habitat, as 'one of the world's great high alpines ... like a white *Eritrichium nanum*, and quite as beautiful'. In cultivation the species has a baffling behaviour. It has been classified as suitable for outdoor culture, and like many of New Zealand's mountain flowers it is accustomed to regular rainfall during the growing season. Response to open garden conditions can, at first, be very promising: growth is quite vigorous under the effects of sun and showers, and flowering suggests that the plant is content. This satisfactory state may continue for months; then, suddenly, blackened and unquestionably dead rosettes appear in the cushion, and unless swift action is taken, the whole plant will pass away within days. Transfer of the stricken specimen to a place under glass can halt the decline, and if the affected foliage is removed, full recovery may follow. There is no clear explanation for this abrupt change in state. It could be that the plant, in youthful vigour, stays healthy even though the frequently saturated condition is not to its liking, but eventually the plant succumbs. Another possibility is that when wetness is combined with high temperatures, the threat from fungal disease is too strong for the plant's defences, hence the sudden onset of trouble.

Although aphids occasionally sample this stranger from a far-off land, they seem to prefer the sap of more familiar victims, and are rarely a problem. Propagation from cuttings is possible, but seed is now becoming more easily obtained in a fresh state, and produces stronger plants.

Myosotis uniflora is one of the exceptions to the preponderance of white-flowered species in New Zealand's flora. This tidy cushion-maker bears yellow blooms in good quantity over its soft and fairly open-

55. *Kelseya uniflora* in its vertical and baking-hot habitat.

structured mound of narrow-leaved shoots. It leads a precarious life on shingle banks, deposited where the mountain rivers lose their pace upon meeting the valley floors. Stronger-than-usual spates can wipe out whole colonies of the plant in a single day.

In cultivation the plant has waxed and waned, and cannot be honestly regarded as safely established. It has a vexing tendency to die, suddenly and inexplicably, after building up a good healthy cushion full of vigour and promise. As it is not a naturally short-lived plant we must look elsewhere for the causes, and frost may be one of the culprits. Where the foliage is still wet from rain or watering when the temperature falls below zero, it can be turned black and lifeless in a matter of hours. Soil mixtures and composts in use have a combination of sharp drainage and nutritious organic matter in their make-up; typically a blend of leafmould or light loam and grit, in equal proportions. Full light is needed to keep the cushion in character and to promote good flowering. This is not an easy plant to propagate from cuttings; a 10% success rate in striking roots is a notable result. Seed should be as fresh as possible, and even so is very unlikely to germinate with abundance.

It would seem that until we learn more about the cultural needs of these two species, it is safer to house them in a glass-covered environment, even though this is far removed from that of their native mountains. The compost most often employed contains roughly equal proportions of grit and humus-rich organic material. Perhaps we are wrong in this respect, and that a significantly different compound would improve matters, but it has yet to be found.

Nassauvia gaudichaudii

A curious and unusually formed cushion plant from the Falkland Islands, far from any mountain habitat, it grows in poor soils comprised of sand and peat, on coastal heathlands, fully exposed to all the elements. The branching, woody shoots terminate in dark green, open rosettes of pointed leaves, armed with little translucent spines, to create a quite dense, low mound. In June many of the rosettes produce totally sessile flowers in twos and

56. From the bleak coasts of the Falkland Islands comes *Nassauvia gaudichaudii*.

threes from their leaf axils to give a respectable covering of bloom on the cushion, but in doing so reveal a very odd aspect of behaviour. The five creamy strap-shaped petals of the flower are not all put out together, but emerge irregularly, the last one delayed for a few days! The lop-sided effect thus produced gives the display a slightly bedraggled look, but does little to detract from the plant's charm.

The term 'bone hardy' has been used more than once to describe the constitution of *N. gaudichaudii*, which is no surprise in a species capable of surviving the harsh weathers in the approaches to Antarctica. In the garden its toughness equips it well for our British winters and erratic growing seasons, and it should not be pampered, otherwise it may be killed by kindness. The main essentials in cultivation are good, sharp drainage, lean, acid soil mixtures and an avoidance of hot, dry positions. Excessive shade or rich compost will promote soft, lank growth and little flower. In most of Britain the plant should stay in good condition and retain its natural character without any form of protection. Cuttings of healthy shoots, taken in August, can be expected to root well and be strong enough for transfer to small pots of gritty compost before winter sets in. Good seed has come into our hands of late and new stocks of young plants are increasing the availability. Plant this tough little islander in a scree open to the sky, but not broiled in high summer, and it will probably thrive for many years.

Petrocallis pyrenaica

Strange that this beautiful crucifer should be so closely identified with the Pyrenees, as though those mountains were its only or at least strongly favoured home, yet it is abundant elsewhere, in the Alps, Dolomites and further eastwards as far as the Carpathians. It is an inhabitant of limestone rocks and screes at the higher levels and is rarely found growing in any shade. Spring transforms the grey resting cushion into a fresh-green mound covered in neat, full-petalled flowers of soft lilac,

57. *Petrocallis pyrenaica* in a limestone niche.

58. American phlox cultivars are often spectacular – *P.* 'Crackerjack'. (R. Rolfe)

with a pleasant vanilla fragrance. In rubble the growth may wander round the larger cobbles, but where the anchorage is on fine scree or a fractured face of rock the low domed shape prevails.

It is less seen as an exhibit than it deserves to be, possibly because it has a listless response to being grown in a pot and does much better in the open garden on a scree or a tufa boulder, in an open, sunny situation. If the winter is very wet, a pane of glass propped over it may help to keep the cushion in good condition, but in general the plant is not demanding.

A contented garden specimen may seed around in a restrained way, but for routine propagation cut out a few strong shoots after flowering and root these in moist sand using a conventional propagator.

P. pyrenaica is occasionally listed by nurseries specializing in alpines and there is little risk of getting a poor form as the species has no great natural variation. If the plants offered have their flowers anything more than slightly above the foliage, or if the cushion is not tight, it is likely that they have been reared in insufficient light and not that it is an inherent flaw in their character.

Phlox

To do them justice as quality cushion plants, a select few from the many low-growing American phloxes have to be mentioned, but unfortunately with some reservations. On their home ground, in the mountains of North America, certain species have developed tightly grown hummocks which they smother in flower, but in our low-altitude garden conditions, no matter how much light we give them, they become lax and drawn. Instead of cushions we have soft heaps of elongated shoots, and although these produce blooms of the right size and form, their quantity is lacking and the whole effect is one of impoverishment. Growers in other European countries with more intense sunlight in their summers do better; the plants are more compact, yet still fail to match those in the wild. For anyone who relishes a challenge, however, there are three which

59. Rare in cultivation is the American *Phlox hendersonii*.

offer great rewards to the successful cultivator.

Phlox condensata (syn. *P. caespitosa* var. *condensata*) is a plant of alpine tundra regions, in a number of locations including Montana, New Mexico, California and Oregon. This is a very compact species, considered by many American rock gardeners to be the best of the cushion types. Its flowers vary from white to pale blue in the colonies, and sit flat on the foliage.

Phlox tumulosa is described in some references as having the tightest cushion in the genus. Restricted to a few sites in east-central Nevada, it is categorized as a rare plant in the wild. The flowers are white, sessile and have a delicate paperiness in their petals.

Phlox hendersonii is essentially a larger version of *P. tumulosa*, with the exception of its flowers, which are almost identical in colour, size and form.

In cultivation the type of compost used does not seem to be critical. Excellent drainage is essential, and to this end one half of the mix should be grit or fine chippings, the remainder needing only to contain a reasonable proportion of nutritious material in its organic make-up. Very lean composts, used in the hope of encouraging compactness, fail in this respect, and unless liquid feed supplement is given at intervals will only starve and emaciate the plant. There is nothing helpful that can be added to these few points; success still eludes us. Detailed information regarding the behaviour and habitats, which might help us to improve our cultural results, is in very short supply, and we look westwards for aid.

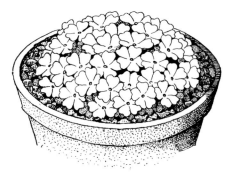

Primula allionii

Of all the hundreds of species in the genus Primula, and of all their great variety, only one, *P. allionii*, grows as a cushion. Its home is in the lower limestone formations of the Maritime Alps, and only in a few restricted locations, particularly where the rock is a fairly soft conglomerate of limestone rubble cemented together by a tufa-like substance. The wild plants make an astonishing sight on shaded cliff faces and cave entrances, utilizing the tiniest of crannies and clinging in every possible attitude, even inverted beneath overhangs. Crumbling perches and other natural hazards prevent many of them from achieving neat forms, but in favourable spots they grow as uniform domes of tightly-clustered, sticky leaf-rosettes. The glory of their flowers comes early, in March and April, dependent on the altitude of the location, and earlier still in cultivation. The colour ranges from rose-magenta, through a host of pinks and mauves, to pure white, and so prolific can

60. *Primula allionii* forms a true cushion.
61. *Pygmea pulvinaris* (syn. *Chionohebe pulvinaris*) takes time to reach its flowering potential (opposite). (R. Rolfe)

be the flowering that the plant becomes a little hillock of solid bloom.

The growing conditions which satisfy this primula in captivity are at odds with those sought by the wild plants. Composts used are quite rich, by crevice plant standards, and ridiculously so when compared with the inhospitable, soilless cracks in which *P. allionii* thrives in nature, yet they result from years of successful cultivation. John Innes potting compost mixed with an equal bulk of grit produces good plants, as does a blend of leafmould, loam, coarse sand and limestone chippings, in equal quantities. Although many attempts have been made to grow plants in the rock garden, the results have been disappointing, but in the alpine house the quality of growth and flower rival those in the wild. Botrytis mould is the scourge of *P. allionii* and the skill in keeping it healthy lies mainly in strict control of moisture content in the compost, to maintain a level which is just adequate for the plant's needs, plus vigilance in the detection and removal of dead and dying leaves before they become a focus for mould growth.

Propagation holds few problems: the plants produce seed in cultivation and can also be vegetatively increased, either by cuttings or division.

This primula is by nature very variable in vigour, compactness, leaf size and form, and above all in its flowers. As a result there has been a lot of selection and naming of horticultural clones, some originating in the wild, but many raised from home-produced seed. To give some idea of the range, I present the following selection.

P. allionii 'Anna Griffith'
Of wild origin and forming a tight cushion of bright green, toothed leaves. The delicate pink flowers have notched petals.

P. allionii 'Celia'
Consistently produces flowers with seven or eight petals in a strong lilac pink. The leaves are a rich green.

P. allionii 'Crowsley Variety'
A slow-growing form with deep, rich crimson flowers over grey-green, small-leaved cushions.

P. allionii 'Avalanche'
Raised by the eminent plantsman Joe Elliott. Slow in growth and compact, with white flowers bearing scalloped petals.

Pygmaea pulvinaris
One of the first of the many fine New Zealand cushion plants to become valued and established in British rock gardening. Not to be coddled and fussed over, it revels in climates which give it regular showers of rain and dislikes only parching conditions. It is without doubt an alpine species, coming from the Southern Alps, making its home at heights around 2000

m (6500 ft). It becomes energetic as soon as it emerges from the melting snow and hurries to bloom, pushing up numerous white, sessile flowers, with fat, starry petals, from its furry and sombre cushion.

There is not a lot of effort or skill involved in keeping *P. pulvinaris* healthy and attractive. Gritty but humus-rich soil mixtures, with no significant lime content, suffice for trough- or pot-grown plants and a rich, acid scree bed is equally suitable. Although some growers insist that winter protection is not essential, the splendid specimens seen at shows and exhibitions enjoy shelter from the wet whilst they are at rest, but at no time during this inactive phase are they allowed to dry out at the roots. Dry periods during the growing months are the times when water should be supplied unsparingly, and if possible daily, to prevent distress to the plant.

Cushions improve in their inclination to flower as they mature, but never really approach the quality or quantity of the display in nature. The tendency is for the flowers to congregate in a patch on the crown of the cushion, and they have a crimped look about them that is not seen in the wild.

The popularity of this species is evident in its regular availability; never in large quantities, but almost always offered each year by one or other of the better alpine nurseries.

Sagina boydii

The reader might be surprised to find a 'pearlwort' amongst the alpines in this book, especially if he or she has a garden cursed with the one that makes little mossy mats and has an inexhaustible determination to take over every bed, trough and pot, but this is a quite different species – or is it a hybrid? Its origin is uncertain; it is believed to have been found by that eminent Scottish plantsman William Boyd, in 1887, during one of his many excursions into his native hills, yet never to be rediscovered despite many diligent searches.

The flowers of *S. boydii* are minute and unimpressive, but the cushion is a thing of wonder, composed of irregularly shaped leaf-rosettes of a deep, rich green, and so shiny that they might have been french polished and kept up to standard by weekly burnishing with wax and duster.

Every plant in existence has come from the original and unique specimen; each one a cutting from a cutting from a cutting ... for over a century of propagation. It still survives, in limited numbers, but not too few as to make it impossible to obtain. It is no miff: its constitution is strong enough for outdoor life, where it is far better grown, as it is a martyr to red spider mite when kept under glass. Cuttings root with little difficulty in moist sand, but should be given extra time to develop a substantial amount of root before being transplanted into their permanent places. The drainage must be faultless and the compost or soil mixture needs at least half of its make-up to be grit or fine chippings. A placing where the sun smites hard may inflict damage to the foliage, hence light shade is advised, just for the hottest part of the day.

Saxifraga oppositifolia ssp. rudolphiana

This little gem has been kept separate from the saxifrage groups, for it belongs to none of them. The straight species, *S. oppositifolia*, has to be one of the world's greatest and best known alpines, circling the entire Northern Hemisphere in its distribution and in all its haunts, growing

62. The jewel-like flowers of *Saxifraga oppositifolia* ssp. *rudolphiana*.

as a creeping mat. In contrast ssp. *rudolphiana* is confined to the Austrian Alps and occurs there only in scattered, small colonies, but its major distinction is its form: tiny shoots of emerald green are packed as tightly as they can possibly be in a smooth, low cushion. No creeping stems emerge to spoil the symmetry; the little mound just expands slowly with the years, building a core of compressed and preserved old foliage, as solid as moorland peat. The natural locations are open and sunlit, and within them the plant is found growing in two surprisingly different substances, either on outcrops of soft schist, or in rock clefts containing peat-like accumulations. Superficially the schist appears rather arid, but in fact is so openly granular in structure that it holds moisture well, and its friability allows the saxifrage to send fine roots far below the surface. In both cases, therefore, there is a reliable water supply. The flowers of this dwarf are astonishingly large, almost reaching the size of those borne by *S. oppositifolia*; they sit directly on the cushion, giving it a crown of carmine-purple.

As a cultivated plant ssp. *rudolphiana* is uncommon and something of a connoisseur's item, yet there are no good reasons for this exclusiveness. The rarity and reputation for difficulty may be the result of growers giving the plant (understandably) the treatment suitable for *S. oppositifolia* and other scree/crevice species. Experience, consisting mainly of trial and error, has shown that the needs of this subspecies are much closer to those of the New Zealand raoulias, which means 'high-fibre' composts or soil mixtures and a love of summer rain. This is convincingly demonstrated by a garden specimen in north-east England, which has for several years now remained healthy, increased steadily and flowered in character. It grows in one of the peat blocks edging an ericaceous bed. In this instance no protection is given to the plant, but it does enjoy a little shade from the hottest sun. Drought is the main enemy, and its damaging effects take time to show; it can be weeks or even months before brown, lifeless patches in the cushion, signalling that at some time there was dryness at the root when the plant was stressed by hot weather.

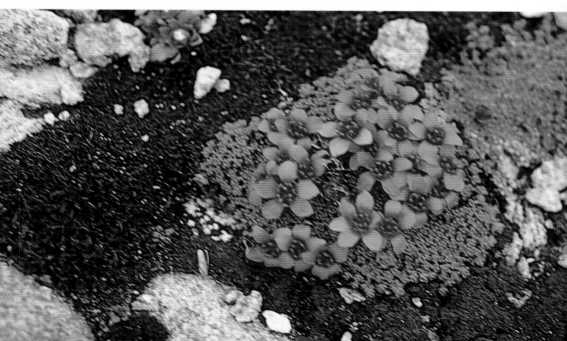

Diminutive forms of *S. oppositifolia* are constantly being mistaken for ssp. *rudolphiana*: they appear on show benches and

63. *Silene acaulis* in its natural home.

in nurseries; also many a treasured seedling turns out to be the wrong thing. The genuine article is hard but not impossible to find, and true seed is sometimes listed by specialist suppliers and rock gardening societies and clubs. Once seen it can never be confused with any other species or form.

Silene acaulis

One of the commonest and most widespread of Europe's mountain plants, which, at its best, competes with the high-level androsaces for spectacular floral display and beauty of cushion. It is found on a variety of rock types, including granites and acid shales, dolomite and other limestones, but must have a place open to the sun for the best of the day if it is to bloom freely. The cushion is rather soft, bright green and composed of crowded, narrow-leaved tufts, from which the little campion flowers rise singly on short stems. In only a small colony the individual plants can vary in flower colour from carmine-rose to delicate shades of pink, and pure white forms occur sparingly in some locations.

The plant has been cultivated for a very long time, and yet well-flowered specimens are scarce, but not for want of selection and encouragement by growers. Away from its mountain home this silene has a fickleness that will have it flushed with bloom in one garden and hard put to flower at all in another, despite both being given the same treatment. Those who have had little success should try a young plant in a block of tufa, placed where it will have a plentiful amount of sun. It will take a year or two to settle down and consolidate its growth, but then it will often start to flower ungrudgingly and reliably each spring, with a long life ahead of it. The latter assumes, of course, that the youngster used is from a parent known to have the inclination and ability to

64. *Silene acaulis*, content on a tufa boulder in the garden.

bloom well when content. The protection of the alpine house, plunge bed or winter cover go unnoticed by this tough and weatherproof rock plant and bring about no better results than the open garden or trough.

The begging of a few cuttings should be a natural response to any discovery of a garden specimen bearing a wealth of flowers; it may be one of those rare, easy-going forms that does reasonably well wherever they are put.

Newcomers to cultivation

There are still regions of wilderness left in the world, holding plants that await discovery, and mountain ranges which have been, as yet, only cursorily botanized. Expeditions are penetrating deeper and more thoroughly into new territories, and as many of these are harsh and semi-barren, the cushion form is not uncommon in the plant life that they contain. New and often unnamed species are being steadily introduced by the explorers and, to their great credit, the collected material is put into the hands not only of the professionals of botanic institutions, but also of a number of amateur growers of proven skill and dedication. The work of sustaining and propagating is thus shared and carried out under a variety of conditions and with differing methods, thus increasing the potential for success and eventual availability.

South America's great Andean mountain chain is full of the unexpected and unfamiliar in its flora. Small, hard mounded growths with beautifully modelled leaf-rosettes are revealed as violas

65. The – as yet – little-known *Oreopus glacialis* of the Andes. (R. Rolfe)

66. A cushion-forming sorrel of the Andes (*Oxalis erythrorhiza*) (below).

only when the recognizable 'pansy' flowers peep out from the compressed foliage. On the high, bleak stone slopes *Oxalis* has none of its usual sprawling or creeping habit, but grows as a dense cushion and flowers even more brilliantly than do the species of lower levels. Currently, most of the plants introduced are native to the southern end of the Andes and the steppe country leading to them, where the growing season is generally cold, frequently windy and beset by alternating scorching and soaking conditions. Few of the plants are proving to be even moderately easy to maintain and a number have a strong tendency to become drawn and out of character. The British temperate climate fails to provide the growth-halting effect of a bitterly cold and early end to the growing season; a normal feature in the natural habitats. Also, any British summer period, which provides what passes for strong sunshine, usually produces in addition a heated atmosphere, which is unnatural for the Andeans and no doubt distressing. So strange, fascinating and dramatic are these New World species, however, that quite certainly the cushion plant enthusiasts will persist in their efforts to cultivate them. Of the many enticing plants discovered only a small proportion have been grown to a reasonable standard or have a fair chance of becoming established, and it is from these that the following have been selected to give the essence of their lure.

Calandrinia caespitosa has celandine-like flowers borne singly on short stalks above a close, succulent cushion, their colour ranging from cream through rich yellow to red/yellow. Typically the plant grows on stable screes saturated by meltwater. Another species, *C. sericea*, prefers much drier sites and has its cushion enhanced with silky hairs. Its flowers are of a deep

rose and tend to be larger (sometimes twice the size) than those of the preceding species.

Chaetanthera spathulifolia was only introduced recently by seed collected on the border of Chile and Argentina at 3700 m (12000 ft), where its broad-leaved, silver-grey rosettes form tight humps and produce their yellow composite flowers to sit on the foliage. The habitat is exposed acid scree fed by snowmelt percolating through the rubble.

Nototriche compacta came to us from lava screes at over 5000 m (15600 ft). It is variable in the formation of its leaf-rosettes (all are attractive) and bears stemless, pink flowers of a shallow goblet form. In cultivation it has so far been disinclined to build up a good cushion and its flowering has fallen short of its display in nature.
N. hartwegii is an Ecuador species with crocus-shaped mauve flowers and has been successfully grown (and flowered) as an open garden plant.

Perezia lanigera was first raised and grown under its provisional name of *P. sessiliflora*. It makes a well-proportioned cushion of stiff-leaved rosettes, each of which looks like a tiny *Lewisha rediviva*, and flowers with small pink 'dandelions' in May. It is a plant of the alpine steppe terrain, growing in peaty soil. Cultivated plants need protection from winter wet.

The rosulate viola has become a symbol of the Andean mountain flora. Not all the species form cushions; some are columnar in habit and certain of them generate new shoots from a woody rhizome in addition to multiplying their rosettes in the normal cushion plant fashion. Of those species presently in cultivation the most

67. A strange, cushion-forming violet of the Andes (*Viola atropurpurea*).

promising cushion makers are *V. atropur-purea*, *V. columnaris*, *V. coronifera* and *V. cotyledon*.

Wernaria humilis is a plant of high-altitude mossy slopes and consolidated moraines, where low temperatures prevail even in the summer months. It can form a very large cushion (up to two metres across) of its dark green, narrow-leaved rosettes, which it studs with daisy-like stemless flowers of (usually) white but occasionally magenta flowers. High temperatures are likely to cause problems in cultivation.

Lithodraba mendocinensis has the look of a dwarf *Acantholimon* and bears white cruciform flowers held close to its cushion. It has been grown to a respectable size in one or two specialist collections, but up to now is reluctant to bloom. Central Andean Argentina is home to this neat and appealing cousin of the drabas.

Xerodraba patagonica has the reputation of being the slowest-growing of all cultivated cushions, making an average increase of no more than 1 cm (⅜ in) per year. The miniscule, scale-like leaves are clustered in rosettes of barely 2 mm (³⁄₃₂ in) across and the white flowers struggle to open clear of the foliage. In its habitat of alpine steppe this species sees little rainfall after the first few weeks of the growing season and the general conditions have much in common with those endured by arctic-alpine flora.

Cultivating the Andeans

The following relies heavily on the work done and observations made by Robert Rolfe, whose short but intensive field work in the Andes and perceptive studies of the plants in cultivation underly this valuable information.

Many of the South American cushion plants have a tendency to flower relatively late in cultivation, compared with alpines from other regions; they seem to respond to a greater intensity of light, and few are in bloom before May. Also, in the wild, cushions may fail to flower in certain years. This can be a consequence of a generous blooming and seed setting in the preceding year having sapped the strength of the plant, or it might indicate an inadequacy of moisture at the critical time of growth, if the region is one with low or uncertain rainfall.

Cushion plants of semi-desert areas of the Andes root to extraordinary depths. A number of them occur on windswept terraces and bleak slopes of volcanic rubble and ash, through which even heavy rainfall is quickly dispersed and roots must delve far down to reach the residue. The extent of this penetration is illustrated by a report of a small *Astragalus* found in Peru, which was no more than 4.5 cm (1¾ in) in diameter yet had a root system of one metre in depth! In attempts to grow such plants in pots it is usually found that there is a marked vulnerability to rot in the neck and the top-dressing must be carefully and generously arranged to maximize ventilation. Due to their natural response the roots soon emerge from the base of the pot to explore the plunge material, causing serious and sometimes fatal damage to the plant when it has to be moved.

Some of the Andean cushions will accept and even appreciate being exposed to the weather whilst they are active, but the majority are grown under permanent overhead protection. Unfortunately the covering of glass aggravates the plant's tendency to become drawn and out of character in cultivation, a problem that still seeks a solution. It is very important that the grower should check out any field notes and references for a species that he or she intends to try in cultivation; their habitats are extremely varied, from high and low elevations, hot and dry, cold and wet climates, screes, crevices and tundra. Very few will tolerate significant levels of calcium in the rooting medium and indeed for the most part grow in acidic formations, many of which are of volcanic origin.

We have a long way to go in our understanding of the Andeans and successes are in small numbers as yet. We know, however, that quality of light is a very important factor, that rotting of the plants at the neck is perhaps the primary cause of loss, that we have to cater for the extraordinary rooting depth that many species are wont to produce, and that we must, somehow, prevent them from growing on long past the time of year when they would naturally be discouraged by lowering temperatures and shortening days.

Australasia

The lands of Australasia are still yielding new cushion species, and the prospects for their permanence in our gardens are very promising when we look back at the success rates for previous introductions. There seems to be sufficient similarity in the climates of Britain and New Zealand's South Island to satisfy many of the plants native to the mountains there.

Pygmaea ciliolata has been in cultivation for several years now, but only in small numbers. In character is it very like *Pygmaea pulvinaris*, making a crouched, spreading cushion of tiny-leaved branchlets. The small white flowers are of good form, appearing in late spring or early summer, huddled tightly over the dome of foliage. It is responding well to an open position on a raised bed of rich, acid scree, and although winter cover has been given so far, it is apparent from specimens in other gardens that this protection is not essential.

Raoulia hectori is currently in the care of just a few specialist growers, but it is hoped that propagation will eventually make it reasonably available. In appearance it lies between *R. eximea* and *R. mammillaris*, with minute leaves covered in silvery-white tomentum. The form presently grown makes an extremely tight and disciplined cushion, with a constitution that is no easier to please than those of the two species with which it has just been compared.

Leucogenes aclanii is a quite recent arrival, with a promising and vigorous response to life in captivity. In its juvenile state it bears something of a resemblance to a cushion of *Saxifraga burseriana*, although with an even more silvery sheen to its glaucus, spiky leaves. Some propagation by cuttings has already facilitated a limited distribution to interested growers. Its progress will be of considerable interest, particularly as it shows signs of being fully hardy and weatherproof.

The cushion plants of Tasmania grow in conditions far removed from those that we might regard as typical for the habitats of cushion species. They grow on high moorland, in wet screes, soggy peat banks and even on little 'islands' in bogs, where tree stumps or rocks rise just clear of the surface. They also congregate and merge with one another to form lumpy carpets which can contain several species. So compact and rigid is the structure of these cushions that they can withstand amazing loads and impacts: Brian Halliwell, in an informative article concerning the plants, reports that 'it is possible to walk over them in hob-nailed boots and even to jump up and down, yet leave no imprint'! In the wild colonies the plants will often root down into their own self-made compost of old leaves making up the core of the cushion. This behaviour is sometimes extended when seeds lodge in the foliage and root into the cushion, which subsequently results in the young plant sitting atop the old one and slowly growing over it.

As regards the cultivation of these Tasmanians we again benefit from the knowledge of Brian Halliwell, who advises that even in their homeland the plants are reluctant to accept garden treatment. He recommends an ericaceous type of compost, comprized of moorland peat, grit and loam in equal volumes, the grit and loam needing to be lime-free. Also he advises that the compost should be maintained in a wet condition, if need be by standing the pot in a saucer of water, permanently. In the cooler, wetter parts of Britain it should be possible to grow the cushions in peat beds or rich pockets of an acid rock garden, but such experiments will have to wait until more seed or plant material becomes available to us.

The following describes the five species of cushion which cohabit on the bleak Tasmanian moors. None of them is at all easy to obtain, and their naturally sparse production of seed adds to the problem – which should be a spur and a challenge to the keen cushion enthusiast.

Abrotanella forsterioides is exclusively native to Tasmania and belongs to the *Compositae* family. The flower colour has been variably described as brown or greenish. This species has been secured in cultivation both as a pot subject and a rock garden plant, at Kew's botanic gardens.

Pterygopappus lawrencii is another Tasmanian endemic composite, with a grey-green cushion and very small flowers of white with a green tinge.

Two which also occur in New Zealand are:

Donatia novae-zelandiae, which has an olive-green cushion and five-petalled white flowers of about one centimetre in diameter.

Phyllachne colensoi, of the same race as the Australian 'trigger plants' (*Stylidiaceae*), has a drab-green cushion with tiny white flowers.

The last is *Dracophyllum minimum*, an endemic and expected to be the most difficult of the five to coax into cultivation. It has the largest flowers, 12 mm (½ in) across and white with five petals. Again, the cushion is a dull green.

Few things could be more surely predicted than that this list of newcomers will be out-of-date before it reaches publication; even as this is being typed there are two expeditions returning from China's mountains, doubtless bringing in some new cushion treasures with them.

CHAPTER 4

The practicalities of cultivation

Apart from the shelter that pot-grown plants can be given, the amount of control that the grower is able to supply to their culture is much more extensive than that which is practicable or possible for those in the garden. It is no hardship, with the potted specimen close to the hands and eyes, to check its condition, particularly in winter-time when – even if the pot is not kept in an alpine house – it can be taken there, or indoors, where examination and any treatment can be carried out carefully and in comfort. Stooping and stretching over a rock garden bed in anything less than ideal weather does not encourage the same thoroughness and concentration. The watering of pots can, and in some cases has to be, a highly controlled operation, bearing no comparison with open garden conditions, where the only adjustments possible for the regulation of wetting are the use of glass lids for winter cover and the hosepipe in summer dryness (if permitted); otherwise the saturation, or lack of it, is whatever the weather makes it.

Troughs fall somewhere between the pot and the open garden bed, in that they can be regarded as very large pots or very small raised beds. Their capacity is small enough to permit good control of what goes into them, hence soil mixtures can be closely suited to the specific needs of the occupants. Lack of moisture is easily and quickly rectified by brief use of the watering can, and winter excess can be avoided by fitting covers, creating shelters for the worst of the seasons. Unlike pots, however, troughs usually have to stay in one place and generally hold more than one plant, as do the raised beds, and their residents are there for as long as they thrive or until they outgrow the containment. Those things that the grower can influence are, therefore, fewer than in pot culture but more than in the rock garden.

These comparisons suggest that the topic of cultivation would benefit from division into three sections, serving:

(1) pot culture, with the associated alpine house, frame and plunge bed
(2) troughs
(3) garden beds.

There are foreseeable overlaps, for instance in the matter of soil mixtures, but the three sections are sufficiently distinct for separate discussion, and so it shall be.

CULTIVATION IN POTS
Clay pots

These are as old as gardening, and although almost entirely superceded by plastic types now in the horticultural trade, and to a considerable extent in general gardening, they remain favoured by many skilled growers, especially in the cultivation of choice alpines (including cushion plants) and cacti. Their variety today is much depleted, with many specialized and purpose-made forms seen only as antique specimens, but those which we need are still available. Allowing for small differences in maker's styles, there are essentially three types. The first of these and the most used, is the 'pot', which has a height roughly equal to its diameter inside the rim. Next is a more squat version with the height reduced to about three quarters of the inside rim measurement, sometimes called a 'half-pot'. The third is the 'pan', which is the shallowest, with a height of only half the diameter.

Occasionally the 'long tom', believed by some to be necessary for unusually deep-rooted plants, makes an appearance in an exhibition or show. Its proportions are not consistent, but typically the height is one and a half times its diameter.

In its early life a plant needs only a small volume of compost in which to root and for the types of plants with which we are concerned, a pot of not more than about 7 cm (2½ in) diameter is adequate at that stage. After the first year it is very likely that the plant will have exhausted the nutrients and its roots will be approaching congestion, calling for a move to a larger size. The following year may produce the need for another re-potting, and so on, but at some stage, often upon reaching the 20–23 cm (8–9 in) size, the then quite large pot can begin to

be a problem, in both its weight and height. The use of a half-pot at this point eases the handling, reduces the weight and lessens the depth of plunge material required – a matter which will arise later in this section. Some would argue, however, that the shallower half-pot is less suitable for long-rooted plants, but this is questionable; is the plant really affected by the difference, when neither the pot nor the half-pot allows it to root down to anything like the extent that it would if unrestrained?

The 'pan' is ideal for shallow-rooted plants such as many of the ericaceous species, where any further depth of compost would be unused by the occupant. In the larger sizes the pan begins to have sufficient depth to satisfy a number of cushion plants. However, it should be borne in mind that the reduced volume of compost is quicker to dry and hence requires more frequent watering.

Plastic pots

The range of plastic pots now available includes all the patterns and sizes of the clays plus others. Square types are preferred by most commercial growers for their efficient geometry; the edge-to-edge clustering leaves none of the wasted space that is unavoidable with round pots, and the packing for transport and display is more stable. Amateur growers

Fig. 5 **Pot types and their proportions.**

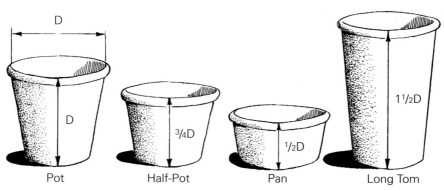

| Pot | Half-Pot | Pan | Long Tom |

have not adopted this new shape to anything like the same extent and hardly at all in the larger size range. A short-coming of the larger plastic pots, whether round or square, is their lack of rigidity, which during handling causes flexing and consequent disturbance of the contents. Careless lifting can result in a sudden cracking of the rim, and exposure to sunlight causes embrittlement in many of the makes. The more expen-sive types with a turned-over rim are superior in strength and far less prone to failure. Some manufacturers put huge drainage holes in their pots, which permit gritty composts to trickle through. These are best avoided unless the grower is prepared to roof over the outlets with crocks. The reason for such generous hole sizes lies in the current techniques used to reduce water-ing chores in nurseries and garden centres, where capillary matting is employed as a wet base upon which the pots stand to take up water and nutrients through their drainage holes. More of this under the heading 'Watering' (pages 119, 124, 128).

The differences in behaviour between clay and plastic pots create the need for modifications to the traditional methods of use. Clay pots shed surplus water not only through the drainage holes, but also through the pores of the material, and evaporation assists the process over the whole surface. The plastic pot has no such porosity and can only lose water by run-off through the drainage holes and some evaporation from the soil surface; thus it retains moisture far longer than its clay counterpart. This can be both an advan-tage and a disadvantage, for whilst reten-tion reduces the need for watering it can also maintain an over-wet condition long enough to harm the plant, unless steps are taken to lessen the holding action in some way. Extra drainage material added to the soil mixture promotes improvements to the shedding of excess water from the pot contents, but the major remedy is a careful watering routine, which can only be perfected by trial and error or a series of methodical tests. Results achieved by growers who have converted to plastic pots leave few doubts that what can be grown in clay can be grown just as well in plastic – when the necessary technique has been mastered!

Peat pots

An innovation which uses compressed peat moulded into pots which are intended for the raising of young plants. Because it is made from an organic and natural rooting medium the pot becomes progressively absorbed into the root-ball, and thus goes with the plant to its potting-on or planting-out. There is very little use of these in the culture of alpines, for in order to act as they should the peat pots must remain saturated and that makes the contents far too wet for these plants.

Plug trays

These have come into wide usage lately and are very effective in the initial raising of seedlings and cuttings. They are made by extruding thumb-sized depressions into light plastic trays to create a multi-tude of tiny 'pots'. The developing roots bind the small volume of compost into a 'plug' which, when firm, can be easily extracted with minimal disturbance to the plantlet, which is then immed-iately ready for potting or planting. They are, perhaps, more useful to the commer-cial grower handling plants by the thou-sand, but deserve attention from the amateur.

Cleanliness

A final observation in the comparing of clays with plastics is the ease with which the latter can be washed for re-use.

Old crusted compost, algae and lime deposit slide off the impervious, smooth surface of plastics, given a sponging with warm soapy water. For the clays, comparable cleansing needs scrubbing brushes, pan scourers and much more time. Badly encrusted pots are hardly worth the effort. Ingrained but light lime coatings, which often disfigure the clay pots of plants grown for exhibition, can be 'ground off' without excessive effort, using 'wet and dry' abrasive paper and water.

The pot and its plant

Few would disagree that life in a pot is far removed from the natural manner of growth for any plant, and the more so for those species like the cushions with specially developed, far-reaching root systems. These, when confined to a plug of soil and grit within a solid containment, are unable to range beyond a fraction of their intended reach. Instead of developing the searching web or delving thongs of root they have no option but to circle and intertwine to the point where, in caring hands, they must be moved (repotted) to a slightly larger prison, which gives them a little freedom, but subsequently becomes just as restrictive as before. Applied to us this would be regarded as a form of torture, and some plants react much as we would, yet, amazingly, many tolerate this unnatural state, albeit to varying degrees, and these we can influence by our treatment of the individual plants.

Drainage is the first step in the process of potting, and generates some argument about the need and form of it. Traditionally the clay pot is prepared by bridging the outlet hole with a few shards of broken pot (crocks) or a single shard covered with small chippings. The purpose of this 'crocking' is to prevent blockage of the outlet hole by presenting a much larger area, with numerous escape channels, to the base of the compost. Some growers use a piece of plastic mesh or perforated zinc in place of the single shard and cover this with a shallow layer of coarse grit, but the effect is the same. Critics of this method hold that if the compost is itself adequately free-draining, water will find its way out of the hole without assistance, and that no blockage should build up. Witnessing the care with which so many of the skilled growers prepare their pots (with crocking) it is clear that the critics are still in the minority. Plastic pots, with their multiple and often larger outlet holes, offer many more exits to escaping water and the likelihood of a blockage is far less, hence in the smaller sizes the compost is usually put straight into the pot with no preparation. Many of the larger sizes have outlet holes big enough for compost to trickle through and crocking returns, in a different role, to prevent such loss, often taking the form of a layer of pebbles, covering but not blocking the holes. This is not done where capillary watering is used (see later).

Potting composts would be numbered in hundreds if every successful grower's 'special mixture' were to be put on record. Thankfully, most of the lore and mystique that the subject attracts has, in the past few years, been discredited, mainly by the convincing results achieved with a few simple mixtures. This rationalization has been the work of some skilled cultivators determined to show that complexity and precious mixtures are not essentials to success.

Some detail has already been given, in the plant descriptions, regarding suitable soil mixtures, but here we are dealing specifically with those for pot-grown subjects, which because they can be very closely controlled are less of a compromise than those prepared for garden beds.

Leaving aside for the moment the presence or absence of lime in the materials used, it should be possible to satisfy almost all of the cushion plants mentioned in this book with three mixtures. Before specifying these, however, it is important to identify very clearly the materials involved and to clear up any ambiguities that may have crept into this text so far.

There is really no difference between a 'soil mixture' and a 'compost', but as the latter is part of the familiar term 'potting compost' it will be used exclusively from now on, leaving 'soil mixture' to describe the bulkier preparations for garden beds. Grit, gravel and small or fine chippings can be confused and have perhaps been too liberally used already, so by way of an apology and to help the reader, here are some non-technical but hopefully realistic definitions.

Grit is usually a product of stone crushing, although it can also be from natural deposits. It consists of variously sized granules, ranging from about 3 mm (⅛ in) down to coarse sand, or in everyday terms from the size of a lentil to a grain of sugar, with all the grades in between.

Chippings come in several grades, each of which is uniform in size. For potting composts only the smallest of these are suitable i.e. 3–4 mm (⅛–³⁄₁₆ in) and usually referred to as 'fine'.

Gravel is hard to separate from chippings, the only conspicuous difference being that the stones in gravel are usually rounded whereas chippings are invariably angular. The useful sizes are as those for chippings.

Sharp sand is regularly confused with grit, having more or less the same size range, but should have only a little of the larger material in its make-up, if any. 'Coarse sand' is another name for the same substance.

All of these can be obtained in calcareous and non-calcareous stones, but as it is easy to add lime, but impossible to extract it, the wisest course is to work with the non-limy granites, quartzites and flints.

John Innes compost is intended to conform to carefully established standards of content and quality; however, with the disappearance of authentic 'loam', soils are now the substitute material and are, to say the least, variable. As a result quality and consistency have suffered. Growers outside the UK are not familiar with the John Innes formulae, nor can they obtain commercial product, hence it will be informative to them, and a general reminder, to give the details here.

John Innes No. 1 potting compost is made up of the following, using volumetric measures:

- 7 parts sterilized loam (preferably with a pH near to 6.5)
- 3 parts peat
- 2 parts grit or sharp sand

Added to each bushel of this mixture (37 litres) are: ¾ oz (18 g) of ground chalk or limestone and 4 oz (100 g) of John Innes base fertilizer, which is composed of: 2 parts superphosphate of lime, 1 part sulphate of potash, 2 parts hoof and horn meal (not bonemeal) – all by weight. The No. 2 grade has twice the amount of base fertilizer and the No. 3 has three times the amount.

The much-used abbreviations for these are J.I. No. 1 (or 2, or 3), or even J.I.1 (or 2, or 3).

It is hardly surprising that few amateurs manufacture their own J.I. composts and rely on commercially produced material, usually trying several brands before finding one that is satisfactory and consistent.

Leafmould, to be precise, is the dark soil-like deposit beneath decaying leaves, but the great majority of growers in the UK use what is actually leaf litter, which is the stage of decomposition prior to the final leafmould and looks like spent tea leaves. Although a lucky few have sources which are free from harmful fungi or creepy-crawlies, many take the precaution of disinfecting the collected material before using it. It should be remembered that in Britain the removal of leafmould without the landowner's permission is theft and carries the appropriate penalties! Safer perhaps to produce leafmould at home by stacking autumn leaves for two or three years. Disinfection is achieved by some ingenious methods, including steaming, baking, scalding, chemical treatment and even microwaving. Oak and beech leafmoulds are the most favoured types, but bracken litter has also been used with success.

Peat can come from sphagnum or sedge bogs, the former being more fibrous and acidic. Sedge peat contains much more finely-sized material and can have pH levels approaching neutral. Both have their advocates and are used by some growers as substitutes for leafmould. The very recently marketed peat alternatives, such as coconut (coir) and other processed wastes, have yet to be adequately used and tested before any firm comment can be made.

With the nature of the raw materials now familiarized, the three composts mentioned earlier can be given full attention. Wherever possible, alternative and substitute materials are included.

The '**general compost**', as it can be called, is perhaps the most widely used in the cultivation of cushion plants, and is the standby whenever there is uncertainty as to what the plant needs. It could hardly be simpler to prepare or to remember, and is:

■ Equal volumes of John Innes potting compost and fine chippings (or grit)

For young plants this compost is best prepared using J.I. No. 1, which has the lowest fertilizer content and is least likely to over-feed. Larger plants may benefit from the extra nutrient in J.I. No. 2. If in doubt, stay with No. 1; more food can be given later as required.

The '**strong compost**' is richer in organic content, and suited to those plants for which the general compost is too low in moisture-retentive material, or too quickly exhausted. It is made up of:

■ Equal volumes of John Innes potting compost, leafmould and fine chippings (or grit)

Peat or bracken litter are acceptable substitutes for the leafmould. The J.I. compost can be No. 1 or No. 2, dependent on the maturity of the plant concerned. In cool, moist climates this compost may prove to be too retentive of moisture if used in plastic pots; if so a 50% increase in the chippings should ease the problem.

The '**lean compost**' has only a small component of organic material, hence the amount of retained moisture is low. Plants grown in this superbly-drained compost require diligent attention to their watering. Its use is mainly confined to those high alpine or exposed crevice and scree-dwelling species that find the other composts too moist or too rich, and in consequence become more prone to rot, or grow coarse and flower poorly. *Androsace* and *Dionysia* are typical of the types of plant that, in the long term, may fare better in this spartan mixture, growing more slowly but sustaining good health and flowering more profusely. The usual blend (measured in volumes) is:

■ 3 parts fine chippings, and 1 or 1½ parts of leafmould

The more generous leafmould content might be necessary where the local climate is fairly dry or subject to lengthy dry periods. Grit, if it contains a high proportion of the larger granules, is an alternative to chippings. Peat has been used successfully as a substitute for leafmould, with a tiny amount of low-nitrogen fertilizer added to compensate for its lack of nutrient relative to leafmould.

None of these composts should be regarded as absolutes. Local conditions and the grower's own methods of cultivation may create the need to modify the proportions of the ingredients slightly. It is purely a matter of trying and, if necessary, adjusting them, by degrees, until they produce the best results in the particular circumstances.

Tufa, crushed into crumbs, has been used as a replacement for the grit in potting composts and as a supplement to them. A generation ago it was held in high esteem as a 'special' ingredient capable of sustaining very difficult species which shunned the normal composts. But time and experience has shown it to be rather overrated, yet it can be useful as an extra component in the mixture for dionysias and the like.

Potting-on, or repotting

The basic methods and practices for the potting of cushion plants are no different than those used in general pot culture, but the high levels of grit or chippings in some of the composts make repotting rather

more difficult, with the tendency of the root ball to collapse during handling. The initial removal of the plant from its old pot follows normal procedures, but the transfer to the new one is a delicate operation and can be eased by special assistance. Figure 6 shows how a trowel can be used to cradle the unstable root ball during its move. For this aid to work satisfactorily the new pot must already have any drainage crocks in place and a layer of compost of the correct depth, so that when lowered into its new pot the plant ends up at the right height relative to the rim, without any need for further risky adjustment. The critical depth of the compost/drainage layer is easily determined by sitting the old pot in the new one and adding or removing compost.

Repotting becomes necessary when the plant's roots are overcrowded and no longer able to function properly, but judging the state of a root system within a pot is no easy matter, and only experience develops the skill. There are some rough checks that can help a little; try pushing a plant label down between the pot and the compost and if there is more than the expected resistance, it may be caused by a mat of roots circling the pot, in which case repotting is overdue. A root or two emerging from the drainage hole(s) can indicate congestion, though not always, as some of the deep-rooting species will

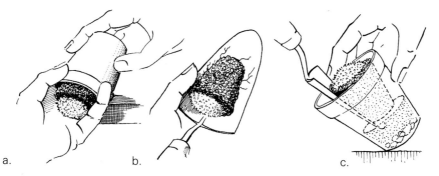

Fig. 6 Repotting: (a) knocking out; (b) cradling the root ball; (c) placing in the new pot.

hurry downwards before they have fully explored the contents of the pot; however, if the escaping roots are forming tassels then it is most likely time for a move. A general decline in the plant's vigour or flowering, combined with a lacklustre appearance, are often indicators of exhausted compost, if there is no evidence of pests or disease being the cause. Once again, it is a matter of insight gained through trial and error and to the newcomer all that can be sensibly said is that if in doubt assume that repotting is needed and do it. If this then reveals that the operation was premature, all is not lost; the root ball, if still intact, can often be carefully eased back into the pot, but if some compost has fallen away then carry on with the repotting. The plant will suffer far less from this untimely upgrading than it would if attempts were made to patch up the soil ball and restore it to the existing pot.

There comes a time when the repotting methods described are no longer valid: the plant becomes too large and too heavy to be held in one hand or to be cradled on a trowel, and knocking the plant out of its pot is a different and awkward operation. A change in technique is required. Such is the weight of the mass of compost and roots that if the pot is tipped through 90°, to stand on its rim, the weight of the root ball will often be sufficient to break its contact with the pot wall. A few gentle blows with the heel of the hand on the pot base will then aid the extraction process. Increasing the tilt and supporting the cushion in a cupped hand allows the pot to be slid away, whereupon the plant can be righted, to sit naked on the bench. At this stage in the operation there is a choice. If the size of the existing pot is at the sensible limit, from the grower's standpoint, some of the root ball can be eased away to reduce its dimensions, allowing a return to the same pot or a clean one of the same size, and fresh compost is then used to refill the space created. If, alternatively, the aim is to transfer the plant to a larger pot then it is very important that the new one is fully prepared beforehand, to minimize the amount of handling, which means that drainage and the correct depth of base compost should be in place. Both hands are then employed to lift and set the waiting plant into its new pot, and this should be a once-only operation; further adjustments to the plant's position can cause serious collapse and damage to the root system. The more swiftly and confidently the move is made, the less will be the risk of failure. Prompt filling in with new compost will forestall any subsequent slumping and all is safe for another year or two.

Whatever the sizes of the pots involved in the operation, there are two conditions which have a strong influence on its success and the extent of any damage caused, both being related to moisture levels. If the plant to be repotted is in need of watering, the soil ball will be virtually dry, or almost so, and in this state will tend to adhere to the wall of the pot. In consequence the soil ball is reluctant to leave the pot and, at worst, may finally come away in pieces or leave a good proportion behind. A plant watered the day before its repotting has a softer and, to some degree, lubricated soil ball, which greatly improves its chances of coming out in one piece, and with less need of persuasion. A very similar extraction problem, in this case confined to clay pots, can arise if the plant was previously potted into a wet, or very moist pot. For some reason this creates a lasting bond between the compost and the pot, which only becomes apparent when the next pot move is attempted. The hazards are essentially the same as those posed by the dry root ball. It is prudent to soak brand new clay pots in clean water for an hour or so, to rinse away any harmful solubles, but then they should be left to dry before use. Easier said than done, of course; most of us must have experienced the mild panic that comes when the de-potted plant is wobbling on one of our hands whilst the other is finding that all the pots within reach are either dirty or wet!

It may have been inferred, in the above, that repotting should always be done as soon as the need is apparent, which would be misleading. As autumn approaches, a plant's growth activity is decreasing, and to repot it in this state, or later, achieves nothing. Little or no root will be made until spring, and the foliage is likewise essentially dormant. The ideal time to move the plant on is during the period when it is busy making root and wanting to develop. In most cushion species this energetic phase follows the completion of flowering, and lasts roughly until the end of high summer. So, if it is late summer or beyond when the plant's need for a move is noticed, it is better left to overwinter as it is, and attended to in the spring.

Top-dressing

The surface upon which a cushion sits is as important to its welfare as the compost in which it roots. In the wild state most of the cushion plants cling to bare rock or fragmented stone, both of which are water-shedding and quick to dry. The neck of the plant, where the stem(s) and the root crown join, and the underside of the cushion are therefore unaccustomed to contact with more or less permanently moist material, which is just what the surface of the compost holds. For the health of the plant it is essential to introduce a much drier, free-draining layer between its base and the compost, which is the purpose of top-dressing, the final task in the potting process.

The conventional method of top-dressing is to spread small stone chippings over the surface of the compost, with care taken to push these well under the cushion and up to the neck. It works well, providing a reasonable barrier to rising damp and allowing air to circulate beneath the cushion through the many gaps and cavities in the chippings – but only if the layer is deep enough. All to often, and particularly in nursery stock, the layer is merely sufficient to hide the compost and far too shallow to function as it should. In small pots the covering depth should not be less than 1 cm (⅜ in) and in larger sizes at least 2 cm (¾ in),

otherwise the 'damp-course' effect is insufficient and invasion by mosses and other low life forms is rapid. Moss, algae, liverwort, and similar invaders progressively clog the breathing and draining channels in the chippings, rendering the top-dressing ineffective. An alternative, which is much less affected by clogging growth and allows more air to the base of the cushion, is to use flakes of stone to cover the compost and to form a 'seat' for the plant. It is hardly suitable for the smallest pot sizes, but otherwise acts more effectively than chippings. Figure 7 shows the arrangement and how, with careful selection and placing, the stone slivers can form a very natural-looking setting for the plant.

A place for the pots

In the early years collections of pot-grown alpines and rock plants were arranged to stand on conventional slatted greenhouse staging, but due to the open and lean nature of the potting composts needed by the plants, the universal use of clay pots and the essentially generous ventilation, drying was rapid. Watering was a frequent event, becoming a more or less daily chore in the warmer weather. The first of the steps taken to improve the system was the replacement of the slatted bench top by a shallow tray containing a layer of gravel, which reduced the air flow round the pots, but made only a small impression on the rate of water loss. Deeper trays, filled with sand into which the pots were sunk almost to the rims, decreased losses dramatically and had the further beneficial effect of reducing temperature fluctuations in the pots, due to the mass and insulating effect of the sand. And so was born the next item to be discussed:

68. Stone flakes provide a near-perfect seat for cushions in cultivation.

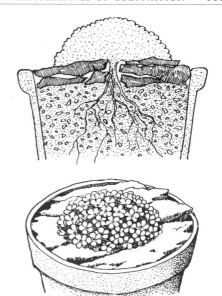

Fig. 7 Flakes of stone forming a 'seat' for the cushion.

The plunge bed

The plunge bed is the foundation of most arrangements accommodating pot-grown plants, and in its simplest form consists of a level area of ground enclosed by (for example) timbers, bricks or concrete blocks, retaining a bed of sand or a mixture of sand and peat. The depth of the filling is sufficient to allow the largest of the pots in use to be sunk to its rim. The ground-level version of the plunge bed is easy and inexpensive to build and has further merit in being directly in contact with the earth; thus in cold periods the ground gives its residual heat to the bed and during hot spells has a cooling effect on the plunge and the pots it contains. The temperature extremes in the rooting systems of the plants are thereby moderated, a cushioning action which is enjoyed by plants in their natural habitats. Another important function of the plunge is the transfer of moisture to and from the pots sitting in it. In the case of clay pots this action occurs automatically, whereas plastic pots must have special preparations made for them. This will be a subject for discussion under 'Watering' (page 119).

It is a waste of labour to excavate the area intended for the bed and to fill this with rubble, in the belief that this will improve the drainage. If the ground is naturally free-draining the water soaks away in any case, and if it tends to hold water then the stone-filled pit will fill up and stay that way, aggravating any problem of over-wetness in the plunge. By laying the plunge material on the existing ground surface excess water must run from it. The only preparation required is the smoothing out of the earth and removal of anything growing in it.

If the bed is to be easily used its access and surround should be clear and smooth. Coarse gravel or lumpy surfacing can be very hurtful to the knees and it pays in comfort if carefully laid paving slabs front the bed. The retaining walls need to be stable and secure if they are to resist the outwards pressure of the bed filling and provide sound anchorage for the securement of the overhead covers. To this end timber requires metal stakes or corner fastenings and brick or concrete walls must be set and laid in mortar. The details of basic bed construction are shown in Figure 8.

Protecting the plunge bed

A transparent roof is still the best protection we can devise for plants which are unable to endure the wetness of our autumns and winters without assistance, and those vulnerable to wet at any time. It is a poor substitute for the crisp snow blanket or dry sub-zero atmosphere of winters to which many of them are adapted and accustomed, yet it allows us to grow to high standards plants that without it would never stay with us. For the simple plunge bed and also those to follow, the protective cover needs only to be easily handled and secured. Glass or clear plastic is held in light frames to provide the covering units, which should be inclined to shed rainwater. The length of the bed has no real limit, but the width is important if everything in the bed is to be accessible. In a bed anything more than a metre wide, the reach across it, from a kneeling position, is not within comfortable limits. Allowing for the thickness of the retaining walls, a safe width for the actual plunge surface is about 75 cm (30 in), but if the bed can be accessed from both sides then this dimension is doubled. Figure 9 illustrates a plunge bed in its single and double forms.

As the figure shows, the front edge of the cover unit rests directly upon the retaining wall and the back edge is elevated on supports, which can be bricks, blocks or a rail as depicted in the double

Fig. 8 **The construction of a ground-level plunge bed.**

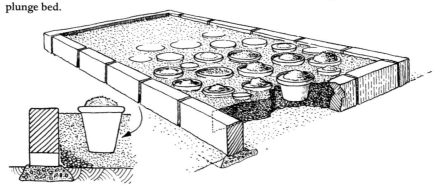

form. The large space thus created beneath the elevated edges is vital for ventilation, as is the triangular gap at the end. If birds, cats or mice are known intruders then smaller-gauge chicken wire can be fixed over the spaces. On heavy clay or other such poorly drained earth it can be necessary to introduce some escape routes for surplus water if the plunge is not to become sodden. Provided that the base of the plunge is not below ground-level (and it should not be), a few thin gaps left in the retaining walls, backed by strips of fine netting, will provide adequate outlets (Fig. 8).

The **raised plunge bed** is a development of the one already described, bringing the working level to a more convenient height and eliminating the need to kneel and stoop. Its structure is much the same as the ground-level version, but with the addition of a firm platform on trustworthy supports, and there are several ways by which this can be constructed. A very substantial type utilizes paving slabs bridging pillars of brick, blocks or more slabs set vertically, all of which involve rudimentary foundations for their stability and strength.

Timber framework is an alternative, but the sections used must be substantial if it is to have the required strength. The foundations, however, need only be load spreaders, and a small paving block beneath each leg will usually suffice. Stout battens, closely spaced on top of the framework, support the floor of the bed, which can be corrugated metal (protected against corrosion) or the plastic equivalent, or exterior grade plywood of 10–12 cm (½ in) thickness.

On the paving-based type the retaining walls are built much as for the ground-level bed, but wood is the most suitable and workable wall material for timber-framed construction. In both cases drainage outlets should be incorporated either in the walls or in the base.

A disadvantage of the raised plunge is brought about by its lack of contact with the ground. This causes it to dry more quickly and to freeze more quickly than the ground-level type. Increased watering compensates for the drying, but little can be done about the freezing, and any plants vulnerable to damage by frosted roots should be housed elsewhere in cold weather.

The covers on any plunge bed are very prone to the dislodging effect of strong winds and in all cases should be fitted with some form of securement. This

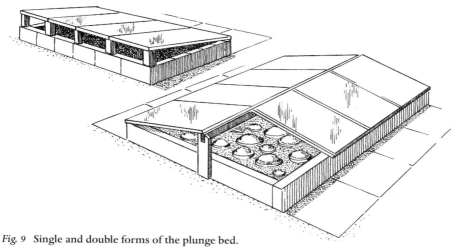

Fig. 9 Single and double forms of the plunge bed.

69. Androsaces in a raised plunge bed.

should be easy to implement. Ropes, wires or weights are troublesome and time-consuming to put on and take off; there is a reluctance to apply these lash-ups on a wet, windy evening and a temptation to just hope that things will calm down. The 2 a.m. splintering crash in a rising gale can be the penalty for such sloth. Simple, quickly-applied fastenings, which need only moments to secure, eliminate doubts and disturbed nights. Figure 11 shows two uncomplicated securements which can be locked in seconds.

As yet the plunge bed has been discussed in its role of winter protection, but

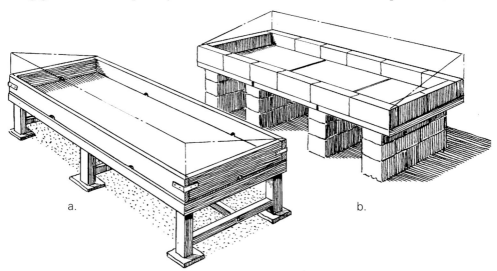

Fig. 10 Raised plunge beds: (a) of timber construction; (b) built with paving slabs and blocks.

it has to function as all-year accommodation for the pot plants and many of them will fare much better, in the growing season, without the roof. By early spring the majority can be uncovered, letting them have the full benefit of the light and refreshment from the rain. Any which cannot tolerate wetting at any time of the year can be grouped beneath one or two retained covers. In this manner the bed maintains its purpose as a permanent home for the plants.

Siting

The siting of the plunge bed is an important matter, taking into account all the elements of the weather and the garden environment. In most cases, once the bed is complete, it is easier to reduce light than to increase it, in the sense that fitting shading is a minor task compared to removing obscuring trees or structures. As many of the plants require full light it makes sense to site the bed, if possible, in a place open to the sun for most of the day and to provide shading for those residents that need it. Other considerations might influence the decision, however, such as exposure to the prevailing winds, frost pockets and areas where moisture and humidity linger, all of which create problems and should be avoided if options exist. Another and fairly obvious detrimental siting is beneath trees or within range of their drips.

Shading

The two ways of creating shade are: to dilute the light or to ration it. An example of the first is the thin colour washing or gauze screening of overhead glass, whereby there is a permanent weakening of the light reaching the plants. The alternative, rationing the light, is achieved with slatted or coarse mesh shades, which allow full-quality light to reach the plants, but for limited periods and in changing places as the sun moves. This system can be employed without the support of overhead glass and is hence more useful for the plunge bed. Colour wash and gauze are normally associated with the alpine house.

A plunge frame?

The shape and function of the plunge bed, as described, might suggest that a short cut could be made by using a conventional cold frame; a ready-made, ready-to-use alternative, but is it? The modern units on the market are of aluminium construction, although a minority of traditional timber types is still available. There is some variety in the action by which the top is adjusted for ventilation and access, but all the models have in common a box-like base with front, back and sides. These are glazed in the metal framed types and boarded in those built of wood. It is feasible that the base could be partially filled with plunge material or, more sensibly,

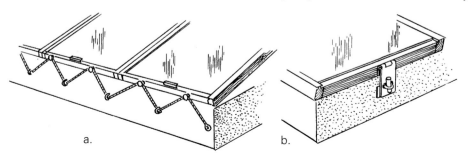

Fig. 11 Simple securements for plunge be covers: (a) using shock cord (bungee); (b) with a hasp and staple.

that the whole frame could sit on a plinth forming the bed, but then the similarity with the plunge bed ends. The cold frame cannot be opened far before it lets in the rain and so the available ventilation is only a fraction of that achievable in the plunge bed, seriously increasing the opportunity for moulds to infect the resident plants. Solid-walled types reduce the amount of light falling on to the plunge by virtually eliminating the side-lighting and are thus liable to draw the growth upwards, creating 'high-rise' cushions with shapes resembling upturned pudding basins. The final comparison is of cost and in this respect the cold frame is the more expensive, and by quite an amount if the plunge bed is of home construction.

Plunge material

Passing reference has already been made to the material in which the pots are plunged, but a little more definition is called for, if only to help in making the right choice. Sand is by far the most widely used plunge filling. It is inexpensive, easy and clean to handle and has the virtue of holding its shape when a pot is lifted from it, allowing a smooth return without need to refashion the hole. This 'moulding' property is most appreciated when the handled pot is within a group. The types of sand are legion and not all of them are suitable; very fine brick-laying sands can have a significant clay content and retain too much water, becoming soggy and almost glutinous when wetted. Coarse sands behave in the opposite manner, allowing a rapid, extensive moisture escape and hence dry out quickly; they also tend to slither into the hole vacated by a lifted pot. The latter shortcomings can be largely corrected, if the granule size is not too great, by adding sieved peat to act as a binding and moisture-retaining agent. Such cautions might seem to make the choosing of sand a diffi-

cult task, but in fact a great range of everyday building sands satisfy the requirements. The best safeguard is to test a sample by filling a pot with it, then watering generously. Note how quickly the sample drains, its consistency afterwards and how long it takes to dry out. Do the same with a similar pot filled with your most commonly-used soil mixture and if the two behave comparably all is well.

Perlite and vermiculite might appear as attractive alternatives to sand. They are moisture-retentive, but not too much so, drain well and are, by comparison, almost weightless, and this last is their downfall. When these are used as plunge material the immediate surface dries quickly, whereupon a mere draught can raise a small snowstorm of granules, the results of which need no description.

The foregoing applies more to the moist plunge system than to the alternative where the sand is kept more or less dry, but in either case an over-fine, poor-draining sand will not act properly. When first making up a 'dry' bed and in subsequent reorganisations, it helps greatly to moisten the sand a little. This eases its packing around and between the pots. Later, when drier, the sand 'sets' just enough to hold its shape if treated gently.

The 'dry' bed system

In use to a much lesser extent than the moist plunge, this alternative is nevertheless just as successful in the cultivation of cushion plants. By its nature it can only be employed under permanent cover and consequently is virtually confined to the alpine house. The plunge material remains dry at all times after the pots have seen set in place and watering is done with a carefully-used, fine-spouted can, pouring into the gap between the edge of the plant and the pot rim. The absence of moisture in the plunge material greatly

70. Cushion plants in the alpine house of a skilled grower.

reduces the possibility of a damp micro-climate building up over the bed, with all the attendant mould problems that this can bring. In its dry state the sand has better insulating properties, but it does tend to draw moisture from clay pots. This action is seen as a safety feature by those who grow species which are intol-erant of the slightest excess in the mois-ture content of the compost.

The alpine house

Perhaps the title is rather grand for what most of us use as a structured shelter for the pot plants. In most gardens it is an ordinary greenhouse, adapted for alpine plants and so referred to as the 'alpine house'. The chief difference between the real thing and the pretender is in the pro-portion of glass panels which can be opened to provide ventilation. With access door(s) excluded, a true purpose-built alpine house has about 30% of its glazing in the form of opening lights; a huge increase to the miserly 3% of the common -or-garden greenhouse, which is inade-quate for most purposes and woefully so for the needs of cushion plants. To achieve sufficient ventilation in the adapted green-house more opening lights or louvres

have to be added, within the limits of cost and practicality. Obviously, the more that can be introduced the better is the result, but it is surprising how effective a mod-erate modification can be. Take for example the most popular size, which is 1.9 m (6 ft) wide by 2.4 m (8 ft) long and normally supplied with just one opening light in the roof. The addition of a second, in the wall opposite the roof light, and another in the end without a door increases the ventilation area to 9%, and this can often be sufficient. Larger houses benefit greatly if they have doors at both ends, encouraging a through draught. Timber-built houses are somewhat easier to modify than the aluminium type, but the latter have much lower maintenance needs. There are arguments about the rel-ative pros and cons, but on the whole, there is little difference in their effective-ness and it becomes a matter of personal choice with a strong cost influence.

The most frequently recommended approach to the use of alpine house venti-lators is to have all of them open all of the time, other than when there are gales strong enough to damage them or risks of in-blown rain or snow. The argument sup-porting this permanent 'wide-open' state is that in the warmer months it acts to cool and freshen the interior of the house and in late autumn and winter it keeps the atmosphere mobile to discourage the growth of moulds. This is sound reasoning for most days of the year, but becomes questionable when those murky or foggy periods come along. Then the thoroughly damp air can drift in and out of the open ventilators and doors, depositing a film of moisture over everything it contacts, creating prime conditions for the spread of moulds. If the house is shut up tight it at least confines the amount of airborne wetness to that trapped within it, and prevents any more from entering. This manner of defence has been put to the test, by the author, for the past three years now, and whilst there have been no dramatic results either way, there are some encouraging indications. The paved floor of the house remains dry, which it never did with the ventilators open, and there are fewer beads of moisture on hairy-leaved plants. These early results are sufficiently convincing to persuade me to carry on shutting out the fog and murk! Electric fans, used to combat stagnation, can do more harm than good if they are drawing in humid air from the outside, but if used to stir up an enclosed atmosphere they are beneficial during the threatening periods of damp weather.

Moving from the structure of the house to its interior, the dominant feature is the staging, upon which the pots are supported at a convenient height for their keeper. If they are clays and merely stand on shallow trays of gravel they must be cared for with great dedication, involving at times a daily round of inspection to ascertain the state of moistness within each individual pot. Sunny days with drying winds make such frequent attention necessary due to the rate at which even large pots can parch if they hold lean, gritty composts. If plastic pots are in use

their drying rate is slower when freestanding, but they heat up far more than the clays, to levels which can be damaging and sometimes fatal to the plants in them; the roots are virtually cooked in a low heat. Sinking pots in plunge to quell such extremes has already been discussed, but the weight of the sand involved is a serious matter. Proprietary aluminium-framed staging might have to be reinforced to bear the load with stability, but the masonry and timber types described earlier for the raised plunge bed are virtually unchanged for use in the alpine house.

The role of the greenhouse as a barrier to frost has little relevance for cushion plants, there being so very few that are at all vulnerable. Some otherwise totally hardy species can have their flowers damaged by freezing, but they hardly warrant the installation of expensive safeguards. Unless the freeze-up is severe and of long duration a short-term covering with a few sheets of newspaper or, better still, a layer of bubble plastic will normally act as an adequate shield.

As yet the house has been considered only as a permanent residence for the pot-grown plants, but it can be used as a temporary shelter. Plants which spend most of their lives in outside plunge beds may be brought 'indoors' at the point of flowering to bloom unsullied in the extra protection, which is also shared by the grower, who enjoys not only the display, but in many instances the subtler scents and floral details that can be missed in imperfect weathers outside. As spring gives way to summer the house used in this way may become almost empty, its visitors returned to their outdoor beds to gain the full benefits of fresh air and light.

Pot turning

An otherwise perfectly-formed cushion covered in flower over only half of its surface and bald on the other is a disappointment to most growers. It happens mainly to plants in houses and frames and much less to those exposed to the more widespread light of the open garden. A cushion that is unbalanced in this way is reacting to having a sunny and a shadowed side. Turning the pot at intervals prevents this one-sided blooming. Using its label as an indicator, the pot is rotated through 90° or so every four or five days in the growing season, and less regularly when at rest. Not all species need this evening out of light, but it is safer to assume that it is necessary until experience proves otherwise.

Watering

It is said that more plants die from over-watering than from any other cause, and whilst this is probably valid for cushion plants during their resting state, there are dangers in being sparing with water when they are active. Even in places with hot, dry summers the spring delivers a flush of meltwater from thawing snow or periods of plentiful rain and the plants respond to this abundance by surging into growth and flower. The absolute drainage of the cliffs and screes prevents any lingering of excess water, but there is always more than enough passing through the rock and rubble to satisfy the thirstiest of the cushions living there. In cultivation the vital swift drainage is assured by the use of open, gritty composts, so however much the plants are watered or rained upon their roots should not encounter soggy conditions within the pots. It is so easy to overlook the rapid drying that can take place on a sunny, breezy day, both in the alpine house and in the plunge bed. If there is cause to wonder if a plant is due for watering it is safer to do it there and then than to carry on pondering whilst the plant may be dehydrating; the excess will soon drain away and the plant will be safe from parching.

As summer progresses there is a lessening of water supplies to many cushion plants in the wild, although those in the monsoon-affected parts of the Himalayas see little reduction throughout their entire growth period. In drier regions the plants there may have to depend upon deeply-held reserves. However, with only a very few exceptions, the cushion plants as a whole do not encounter dryness at their roots in normal circumstances. If they do, as a result of an abnormally dry summer or a poor snow accumulation in the preceding winter, they die. A state of drought can develop in a pot in a surprisingly short time and it rests with the grower to ensure that whilst the plants are active, which may extend well into autumn, the compost is never allowed to become less than moist to the touch. Admittedly this is not a precise gauge, but even using a moisture meter produces readings that vary so much with the type of compost that not even rough guidance figures can be offered with any confidence. The finger-tip test improves with practice and has yet to be bettered, but getting to the compost to apply it usually involves parting the top-dressing and if the plant concerned has spread close to the rim of the pot this can be awkward. In such a case choose a nearby pot of similar size filled with similar compost which can be accessed, and if watering routines have been carried out properly it will serve as a good indicator. Plants in the open plunge beds are frequently saturated for days on end during spring and summer rains, but the open-structured composts prevent the pot contents from becoming miniature bogs; their condition is very wet, but the water is constantly passing through, fresh and aerated, very much as it does in the natural habitats. In this state the plants are overwatered yet safe from stagnation-loving rot. These remarks apply, of course, only to those species suited to the outdoor life whilst in growth.

Late autumn and winter bring the need for tighter control of watering, to cater for the dissimilar requirements of the individual plants when at rest. A rough division can be made between European and Himalayan species, with the Europeans generally comfortable in quite low moisture levels at their roots, unlike the Himalayans which must have something approaching the summer minimum if they are not to shrivel away in their sleep. In the alpine house these needs call for regular attention from the grower, but in outside, ground-level plunge beds the task is much less demanding as, after the covers have been put in place, drying is slow and there is a store of moisture in the plunge material to maintain a steady state for months. In such conditions clay pots are superior in their ability to draw in moisture from the plunge. The plastic type must rely on the much more restricted take-up through their drainage holes and require periodic checking to make sure that the pot content is not becoming dry, even though surrounded by moist plunge.

Exactly what causes a cushion to be enfeebled or killed by overwatering is hard to define. As has already been pointed out, the majority will tolerate excess when they are in growth, though there are sensitive species, like the dionysias, which demand carefully controlled levels at all times, but in the dormant condition many more cushions become intolerant of over-moist compost. It may be that a damp micro-climate forms around the plant, encouraging fungal attack. The plant's defences against disease are almost certainly reduced whilst it is torpid, hence the water-borne assailants which it can defeat when in vigour may then succeed. The effect of frost is greater where the moisture level is higher: the rupture of

cells and the solidifying of root fibres will be more likely in a plant which is given more water than it needs to survive dormancy. A potted plant can become a solid frozen block in a hard frost, and although in its native winters it may be exposed to sub-zero temperatures, it stays frozen until spring, whereas the cultivated specimen probably experiences several freeze-ups and thaws over two or three months. Under these extremes a plant which is just moist must behave differently than one which has been given too much water. One or more of these effects may be sufficient to change the outcome from survival to death if the moisture content of the compost is above a critical limit. No textbook will state what that limit is; it has to be discovered by the grower for his or her particular conditions, methods of cultivation, materials used and the influence of local weather.

The state of the plunge material can have a strong influence on the moisture conditions within the pots that it holds. The compost in clay pots can be assumed to have roughly the same dampness as the plunge, due to the ease with which moisture can pass from one to the other. A few very skilled growers rely entirely upon this process to achieve fine control; using clay pots exclusively, they apply water only to the plunge, never watering the plants directly. The restricted uptake of plastic pots is an obstacle to their being used in this way, absorption being only through the contact of compost and plunge material at the drainage holes.

Watering devices

New materials and technology have given rise to an assortment of semi- and fully-automatic systems designed to supply measured amounts of water to selected points or over chosen areas. For the amateur's modest needs the simpler types can be useful, provided that they are not relied upon too heavily. Changes in the weather alter the day-to-day moisture requirements of the plants, but these unsophisticated systems keep up a fixed rate of delivery unless the grower is there to adjust them. Nevertheless, they can act as a short term 'caretaker' at least to prevent drying out during a few days' absence. High-tech devices, with sensors and electronic control, are capable of responding and adjusting to climatic variations, but are by their cost and complexity beyond the remit of this book.

Capillary matting has revolutionized commercial pot culture. It provides a permanently wet base upon which the pots stand and from which they take up water by capillary action, through contact of the compost with the matting at the drainage holes. Each pot is in effect a 'wick'. As a very short-term watering system it might have its uses for cushion plans, but generally speaking it is unsuitable, as it maintains what is for them an over-moist and somewhat stagnant condition in the compost.

Dribble hose weeps droplets of water throughout its length and the primary applications are for the gentle, continuous supply of water to borders and beds. Perhaps it could be used for maintaining a moist plunge, but it is difficult to see how the rate of flow could be low enough to avoid overwetting.

Drip feed systems are based on the principle of delivering water to selected points through nozzles fitted at intervals along a flexible supply tube, which is connected to a tap or reservoir tank. The nozzle adjustment controls the frequency of the drip and low delivery rates can be achieved. The system has been successfully used by some growers as a plunge moistener, and they have learned to live with the plastic serpents straddling the pots.

Youthful resilience

Once or twice in the detailed discussion of the more taxing species, it has been mentioned that the young are untroubled by frequent wettings in the spring and summer months. In the alpine houses this allows overhead watering, and in the plunge bed the juveniles can be left out in the rain. After one or two seasons of growth, however, the maturing cushions suddenly become susceptible to rot, even if only occasionally soaked. The explanation for this change may be related to the build-up of dead material within the cushion; the more there is, the more stagnant water it holds, and the longer this takes to dry off; long enough, perhaps, for fungal growth to take hold.

CUSHION PLANTS IN TROUGHS
The trough

Farms, smithies, tanneries, dye works and village pumps were all common locations for stone troughs not so long ago. Each trough developed its own shape and size to match its purpose, from giants big enough to take a bath in to midgets no larger than a hat, and all of them are now eagerly sought for a quite different use – by gardeners. But demand exceeds supply and the originals are now far outnumbered by their imitations, the best of which are very convincing in appearance and just as good functionally. There are several methods by which amateurs can produce realistic and perfectly serviceable troughs, which are fully described in two other books of the 'Rock Gardener's Library' series.

Essentially a trough is like a pot, but instead of holding a single specimen its large size allows it to house several. Otherwise it is very similar, in that it is a container specially prepared, filled and positioned to suit a particular type of

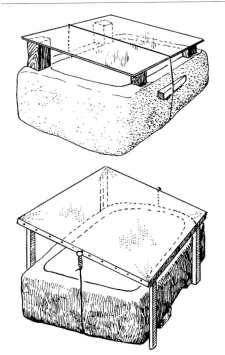

Fig. 12 **Winter covers for troughs.**

compost is less than 12 cm (5 in) deep, long-rooted cushion plants will be badly restricted and threatened by rapid drying out, unless the grower is punctual with watering during arid weather. The drainage must be totally effective and not prone to blockage by fragments of compost and debris washed down into it. An outlet hole smaller than 2 cm (¾ in) diameter is at risk in this respect and should be enlarged.

Siting the trough

The plants selected for the trough are a major influence on its siting and matters are made much simpler if they are all reasonably alike in their environmental needs. For example, a collection of sun-loving cushions will appreciate a fully open site, whereas one which is partially shaded will be more appropriate for a trough of, say, Kabschia saxifrages. Strong, cold winds can be harmful to many cushion species and positions shielded by a nearby hedge or wall will do much to prevent damage. The traffic on regularly-used paths and driveways is a hazard to closely situated troughs; wheelbarrows, lawnmowers and junior cyclists can knock chunks out of them and dislodge their occupants. The flapping burden of the washing line on a breezy day has a whip-like ferocity for any trough plants within reach. These considerations and cautions are worth some thought before beginning what is often the heavy work of moving and setting up a trough.

Filling

The composts described and specified for pot culture are equally suitable for troughs and need no modification, but the preparation and filling process is not quite the same. The drainage hole or holes require crocking just as in the pot, but the hole size is greater and more difficult to bridge. A square of perforated zinc or

plant. In this way alone the trough offers much that a cushion plant requires and it adds to this potential through its form. The strong, solid edges act like the frame around a picture, focusing our attention and causing us to see more detail. In consequence anything that is amiss is noticed early and because in this miniature garden it takes little time or effort to apply a remedy, we tend to do it there and then. As a result the plants benefit from close observation and prompt treatment, as though they were in a special care unit; little wonder that cushions will often respond well to trough culture after being transferred from other growing places where they were failing. Where certain trough residents need overhead protection during dormancy this can be easily provided by simple portable covers, some examples of which are illustrated in Figure 12.

Depth and drainage are the two most critical elements of a trough. If the filling rust-proof fine mesh, cut to cover the hole, is the simplest and most effective solution; otherwise large pot shards or slivers of stone have to be criss-crossed over it. Whichever of these is used it pays then to add a covering of fine chippings which act to prevent compost from blocking the outlet passages in the crocking. There are arguments for extending the layer of chippings over the whole base of the trough, to aid the passage of water to the outlet, but from experience with more than a dozen troughs, some with and some without this bottom layer, nothing conclusive has emerged.

Next to be introduced is the compost, and again it makes sense to select plants which will all find the one mixture acceptable. In small troughs the filling process is hardly different than that used for pots, but in the bigger, deeper ones it is necessary to gently compact the compost at several stages during the work. Leaning on the filling with clenched fists applies the right level of pressure and if this is done after each 8–10 cm (4 in) of compost has been added, the subsequent settlement will not be excessive. Another precaution against the filling being too far down in the trough after a year or so is to make the final level of the compost a little above that at which it is intended to be; the inevitable natural compaction will then, with luck, lower it to the ideal.

Planting

The purpose of growing cushion plants in a trough is to provide them with realistic and encouraging conditions in a space which is small enough to be closely controlled. This is quite different from the convention of creating a scaled-down landscape with slow-growing, dwarf plants and other Lilliputian features. A utilitarian approach that simply puts several plants at reasonable spacings in an otherwise featureless trough will not deter them, but such arrangements appeal to very few gardeners. The pleasing incorporation of a few small rocks need not be purely decorative; it can be artfully combined with the contriving of clefts and crevices to make the cushions feel even more at home. There are two basic ways of doing this, either by laying flattish pieces more or less on the surface or sinking them edgeways into the compost. Figure 13 shows both methods and their effect.

With or without rockwork the planting operation is not just a matter of trowelling out a hole to fit the soil ball of a young pot-grown plant; the roots have to be persuaded to explore the compost of the trough and establish themselves in it. The ever-increasing commercial practice of raising alpine plants (including cushion types) in peat-based composts aggravates the acclimatization of the newcomer to its new home. Roots accustomed to these highly fibrous, spongy potting compounds are reluctant to move out into leaner, gritty stuff unless some fairly brutal persuasion is applied and this involves 'liberating' the roots. As much as possible of the nursery rooting medium has to be teased, tapped, poked and plucked away until a good proportion of the root system is exposed; then planting can go ahead. This applies, to a lesser degree, for plants grown in composts more similar to the trough filling. With the exception of the 'vertical' crevice, planting requires a generous hole to be scooped out, into which the roots can be comfortably spread; then follows a gentle filling in and firming to complete the job. Plants destined for the 'vertical' crevices have to be set in place during the construction, as illustrated in Figure 13. For a week or two following their move the plants need help to recover from their treatment, with diligent attention to

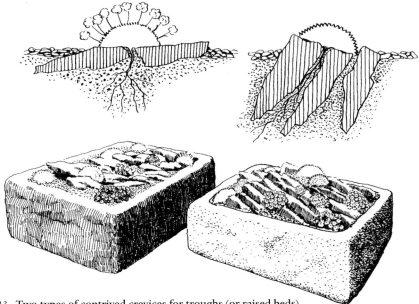

Fig. 13 Two types of contrived crevices for troughs (or raised beds).

watering and shading whenever the weather is sunny or drying winds are about.

The final stage is the top-dressing, which in all respects is the same as for pot-grown plants. Where small rocks have been incorporated it makes a more satisfying arrangement if the chippings or flakes of stone have colour and texture in harmony with the rock.

Watering

It can be quite difficult to judge the watering needs of a trough, for whilst the surface may look and feel dry there might be ample moisture lower down in the filling. Moisture meters, now moderately priced and widely available, are very useful aids, their probes being long enough to take readings well down in the compost. The manual alternative is to find a clear space, scrape away the top-dressing and do a little digging with a slim knife to find the sub-surface state of affairs. If the trough is covered during winter it might need moistening once or twice, although it is not unusual for those of reasonable size to remain sufficiently damp in the root run and to need no attention until spring.

Feeding

Plants can remain as residents in a trough for quite a number of years and the initially available nutrients are usually exhausted after about three years, so further supplies have to be provided. This is done either by liquid feeding at intervals during the growing season or by lightly dusting the trough's surface (but not the plants) with a slow-release granular fertilizer in early spring and leaving it to be washed in by the rain. The latter is the simpler of the two methods and requires only a few minutes work once per year.

Maintenance

The great joy of trough culture is that so little needs to be done to keep everything in order and up to appearances. Occa-

71. **Cushion species on a rock garden mound.**

sional weeds may sprout, but they are soon noticed and easily tweaked out. The odd slug or snail might climb up to look for a meal, but most crawl past, unaware of the plants above. Top-dressing will have to be changed when it shows signs of infiltration by moss and algae, but as this takes about three years to happen it is hardly a chore. Now and again there will be cause to dig out and replace a plant, either because it has become too big or has passed away. Before inserting the successor take the opportunity to revitalise the locality by digging out as much of the original compost, without over-disturbing the other residents, and replacing it with new compost. This will help both the new plant and the general condition of the trough.

Hidden names

All too many well-prepared and planted troughs are disfigured by prominent labels and take on the appearance of a miniature cemetery. If the labels are pushed down into the compost until their tops are just visible the whole appearance is greatly improved, yet the labels can be read by pulling them out a little and the lettering stays on far longer in the buried state.

CUSHION PLANTS IN THE GARDEN

The 'rockery' is no place for cushion plants, save for the lusty, grow-anywhere types, such as some of the mossy saxifrage hybrids. It is more often than not a pile of soil and stones with none of the refinements that are so necessary in the cultivation of these highly adapted species.

Rock gardens are quite another matter; they can feature screes, cliffs, troughs and specially prepared beds, for each of which there are cushions that will accept the conditions offered and prosper, given a little care.

Screes in the garden are nothing like the colossal stone piles of the mountains, but they succeed in satisfying many of the plants from those natural accumulations of debris. The only near resemblance is in the surface, where the garden version looks and behaves something like the real thing and fortunately this aspect is of primary importance to scree plants. The simplest, cheapest and easiest way to make a scree bed is to select an area in the garden which gets plenty of sun and is not apt to become waterlogged in wet weather. If the chosen ground has a gentle slope, so much the better.

72. *Vitaliana primuliflora* is one of the easier
subjects for the scree.

73. The soft-cushioned asperulas have a
froth of flowers when planted in a sunny
scree. (R. Rolfe)

This is then cleared of all plant life
and lightly forked over, just to loosen
the surface and break up any hard-panned
earth. Stone chippings, in the size range
4–6 mm (³⁄₁₆–¼ in) are then laid on the
prepared surface to a depth of about
10–15 cm (4–6 in). The scree is then essentially complete, but it needs an edging
round its periphery to hold in the chippings and this is best achieved with stones
of a thickness roughly matching the depth
of the chipping layer. A few nicely-shaped
rocks, set in the scree in small groups, add
realism and break any severity of the
surface.

Planting the scree calls for a special
technique. The hole prepared for the plant
has to be far wider than would be normal
for a conventional bed, otherwise the
chippings just keep on shuttering down to
refill the small excavation. The plant must
first be prepared much as it is for a
trough, with most of the nursery compost
removed and the roots disentangled.
These are then spread over the base of the
hole and the chippings gently pushed back
into the depression. If the plant is held at
the correct height relative to the scree
surface throughout the infilling, the final
levelling should leave the chippings

touching the neck and supporting the crown. A sigh of relief and the operation is complete – unless the plant ends up too high or too low; in which case either scrape away some chippings and ease the plant down a little, or push a hand fork deep beneath the plant and lever it up a little. From there on regular watering and shading from direct sun for the first two or three weeks after planting are essential to the plant's recovery and establishment in its new, stony home.

A raised bed is simply a walled enclosure holding a prepared soil mixture. The latter term is used deliberately to avoid confusion with 'compost', as for a raised bed the filling material is coarser and likely to be measured in barrow-loads rather than handfuls. The leafmould, peat or other fibrous equivalent is used as it comes, without any sieving, and the chippings or grit are less precise in size, tending generally to be a little larger. Due to the expanse of a raised bed its plant population is rarely confined to one type, hence the soil mixture has to be a compromise for a group of species, which is acceptable to the majority and tolerable to the remainder.

From experience, a 'two-to-one' mixture has proved to be the most satis-

74. A raised bed devoted to cushion plants. (The rail supports winter covers.)

factory for a collection of cushion plants, the 'two-to-one' being shorthand for a blend of:

- 2 parts stone chippings, in the size range 3–6 mm (⅛–¼ in), or a coarse grade of grit
- 1 part leafmould, peat or peat substitute, mixed with an equal amount of high-quality loam or soil

Fig. 14 **The simple scree bed.**

Fig. 15 **A typical raised bed.**

This will also be adequate for other (non-cushion) plants found in the same wild habitats and which might be grown in the bed to provide interesting contrast and form.

Figure 15 shows the construction and main features of a typical raised bed.

Brick, stone, concrete and timber are all used to construct raised beds, but whichever of these is used the structure must be solid and strong. The selection of the site, the preparation of the ground and the ensurance of reach and access all follow exactly the guidelines given for the ground level plunge bed. Drainage has to be catered for by incorporating outlets at the bottom of the surrounding wall, aided by a layer of small rubble and chippings laid on the base. The height of the bed needs careful consideration. High beds are wonderfully easy to work on and their plants are 'in close-up', but they take huge quantities of filling material. Low beds are easier and cheaper to build and fill and don't tower over the surrounding garden. A bed 25 cm (10 in) high is about the minimum for satisfactory results. It pays to remember that settlement of the filling will lower the finished surface of the bed by about 2.5 cm (1 in) for each 30 cm (12 in) of height, after a year or so.

Filling

This operation has many similarities to trough filling, but moves more material and the taller the bed the more arduous is the labour involved. A small cement mixer is a welcome and powerful aid in the making up of the filling material, but the important consolidating of the filling, layer by layer, has to be done by the centuries-old grape-treading method, doggedly and thoroughly. The **top-dressing**, **rock placing** and **planting** are more extensive, but in all other respects just the same as described for troughs.

A raised scree bed is the identical structure filled with an even leaner mixture, comprised of stone chippings and sedge peat or leafmould, in the proportions of: 3 or even 4 to 1.

Watering

Unless of an unusually small size, the raised bed holds a large mass of material in comparison with a trough and so dries out at a much slower rate. In a prolonged summer dry period there should be no need to water the bed until after a week or even ten days of rain-free and sunny conditions. Some growers wait for signs of wilting in the plants before resorting to the hosepipe. When the decision to water has been made it should be done copiously, saturating the entire bed; then it can be left for another week or so before the wetting is repeated (assuming no rain has fallen meanwhile). Supplying water in this generous way and then leaving well alone until it is really needed again is much to be preferred to the frequent but small applications given by watering can or brief spatter from a hose, which tend not to penetrate to the depth where the plant naturally sends its roots in search of moisture.

Maintenance

In terms of upkeep and attention the raised bed is, to all intents and purposes, just an oversize trough. Weeds do not find it easy to seed into the stony surface and hence are far fewer and weaker than they might be on a similarly-sized area of garden soil. Settlement, although allowed for in the filling operation, may not be uniform and some localized subsidence should be expected. Where this occurs a little packing with soil mixture and a restoring of the top-dressing will rectify the fault. The replacement of a plant will be necessary now and again and is carried out in the same manner as it is in troughs.

After several years there comes a slowing down and a lack of zest in the plants inhabiting a raised bed, which no amount of feeding will dispel. The cause is a compaction of the filling: a loss of open structure and aeration; it is 'tired', as gardeners would put it. Then is the time to rejuvenate the bed. This involves taking out and temporarily storing any still young and healthy plants, discarding the old and frail and replacing the soil mixture

entirely; a formidable task, but one which should only be necessary every eight to ten years and the response after the replanting fully repays the effort. If the bed is large the work can be done in sections, over two or three seasons.

Feeding

Beyond the second growing season following the completion of the bed, annual spring feeding becomes necessary, to compensate for the depletion of nutrients due to the take-up by the plants and the leaching effect of the rain. The most direct, labour-saving means of providing it is to apply, in early spring, a slow-release, low-nitrogen fertilizer, at the rate of about 30 g (1 oz) per square metre of the bed surface, taking care not to let it fall on the plants. The rain will wash it in.

CUSHIONS IN CLIFFS

Almost every rock gardener has at some time yearned to own a small cliff or steep-faced outcrop and to populate it with choice alpine plants. A few with the zeal and energy take up spade and crowbar to make the dream come true, but the end result is nearly always a disappointment: it defiantly refuses to look like anything other than what it is – a pile of rocks!

Visits to major flower shows will prove, by superb examples, that it can be done – by expert landscape gardeners using specially-selected materials, but their achievements are only required to last a few days. Some of our eminent gardens, however, feature permanent and highly convincing man-made crags, but they do not have choice alpines filling their crevices and squatting on their ledges; a few sedums or sempervivums perhaps, or some clumps of *Arabis* or *Aubrieta* are usually all that remain from the original enthusiastic planting.

The sad truth is that although mighty

75. A magnificent tufa cliff, of the slab type.

efforts may be made to create a place just like home for the natural rock-dwellers, most of them refuse to live in it. They are washed out by downpours, squeezed out by frosts, tugged out by gales, or simply decline from the day they are planted.

The exception to these failed enterprises is the tufa cliff, which has been developed over the past thirty years and is now a highly controlled and precision construction. There are very few of these in existence as yet, for reasons which will become clear. The tufa cliff has two forms, both of them requiring considerable skill and expense to create. The 'original' form, pioneered by that great alpine gardener Roy Elliott, is built using large blocks of tufa stacked against a supporting wall. To achieve a reasonably close fit, block to block, they are shaped on their mating faces using a saw, so that they marry something like the stones in a masoned wall. A fairly soft tufa is essential, not only to make for easy cutting, but because the plants are grown *in* the tufa,

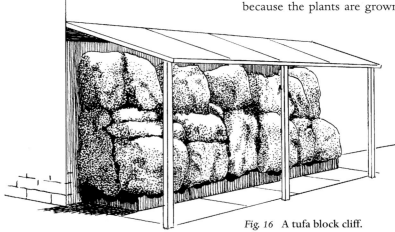

Fig. 16 A tufa block cliff.

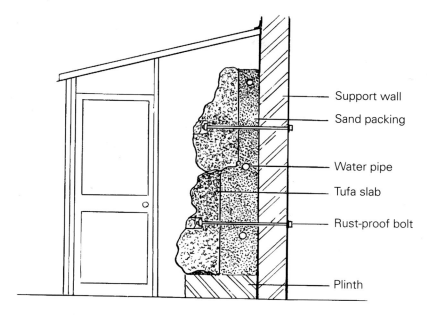

- Support wall
- Sand packing
- Water pipe
- Tufa slab
- Rust-proof bolt
- Plinth

Fig. 17 **A tufa slab cliff.**

planted as small specimens in holes bored in the blocks (see 'Cushions in tufa boulders', page 132).

The latest constructions utilize a by-product of commercial tufa quarrying in Germany. The 'waste' from the process takes the form of slabs which have one face retaining the naturally-formed surface contours and texture and the opposite one sawn flat. A supporting wall is again the 'backplate' of the structure, but from there on the build is quite different. The slabs are set up on edge, in the manner of vertical crazy paving, leaving a gap between the flat rear face and the wall (Fig. 17) which, after the installation of water supply pipework, is packed with sand. In operation, water is fed only to the sand and seeps into the back of the tufa slabs to reach the roots of the plants. Some remarkable successes have been achieved with notoriously difficult plants, and especially cushion types, in this form of cliff.

The watering of both forms of cliff requires special pipework and controls. No natural wetting occurs, as the whole

structure is protected by at least a glass roof and more often is entirely enclosed in a purpose-built glass-house.

A further development is the building of a cliff face with thinner slabs of a hard tufa, and packing the back space with a rooting mixture, such as equal proportions of sand, perlite and vermiculite. Holes are bored right through the slabs, allowing plants to range back into the packing with their roots. Nutrients are added to an automated water supply.

Some hesitation preceded the decision to include the more complex of these cliffs for description, there being much detail in the construction, watering arrangement, planting and aftercare that could not be generalized. Each one is unique: its needs, behaviour and treatment are adequately understood only by its owner. Nevertheless, together they constitute a radical step forward in the cultivation of challenging plants, and hopefully will instigate new approaches and experiments, using other materials and arrangements. These may

76. When grown in tufa, *Arenaria tetraquetra* blooms more freely.

produce simpler, cheaper systems giving comparable results, which is reason enough for inclusion.

CUSHIONS IN TUFA BOULDERS

In addition to being a cliff-building material and a constituent of compost (in its crushed form), tufa has another role in the cultivation of cushion plants, due to its very special properties. Tufa is created by the action of water emerging from subterranean journeys through limestone formations, during which it takes up an abnormal level of calcium in solution. Upon meeting the open air it is no longer able to sustain the limy enrichment, and disposes of the excess by depositing it in crystalline form on whatever it contacts. Where it flows over or splashes leaf litter, moss or other vegetation, these are slowly encased or 'petrified' by the calcium. The same happens to further accumulations of plant debris and so there is a slow build-up of a substance resembling fossilized sponge, which is the form of tufa prized by gardeners. Roots are able to penetrate the soft, porous structure and to exploit the minerals and organic substances entombed in it. The material is naturally free-draining, yet retains moisture in its fabric. For the plants of limestone rocks and screes tufa provides everything they need in a root run and they are well equipped to make the best of it. Kabschia saxifrages are particularly good subjects for planting in a block or boulder of tufa, where they will grow slowly and flower well with the minimum of attention beyond normal watering in dry spells.

To achieve the successful establishment of plants in tufa it is necessary to introduce them when they are still at the yearling stage; then the tufa requires only a small hole to take the root system. Nursery plants, with a well-developed root ball, need an excessively large cavity and in any case have really grown beyond the stage where their transfer to tufa is likely to be satisfactory. In this form of cultivation no compost is involved, nor is there any subsequent feeding; the plant grows entirely in the tufa. Below is illustrated a typical tufa block, set up in a shallow trough with about one-fifth to one quarter of its mass bedded in a mixture of coarse sand and chippings. This base holds the block firm and also acts as a moisture reservoir to some extent. Single or grouped blocks or boulders, in beds and screes, are set in

Fig. 18 A tufa boulder set in a trough. Inset shows the manner of planting.

the same way, but bedded in the soil or scree mixture. The illustration also includes a detail showing the manner of planting.

Where the growth of moss on the surface of tufa becomes a problem it indicates that the conditions are too moist: the tufa is being over-supplied with water, either because it is set too deeply or surplus water is unable to drain away from the base. In such cases tufa behaves like a wick and will keep on taking up water until it is fully saturated.

THE INDOOR ROCK GARDEN

Loosely related to the covered tufa cliff, but with rather more scope for planting, is the raised bed built inside the alpine house. Structurally it is the same as the raised plunge bed, but instead of containing sand and pots it is filled with a soil mixture to provide a common root run for a collection of plants grown 'free'. There is no need for precision in making up the soil mixture. The aim is to produce a rich scree, and it will depend to some extent on local conditions as to how rich it should be, but generally speaking the proportion of organic material (loam, peat, leafmould) is a little higher than would be

appropriate for an outdoor raised bed intended for similar plants. This compensates for the more rapid drying under greenhouse conditions. If leafmould (free from pests) can be had, then a good balance is: 1 part J.I. No. 2, 1 part leafmould and 1½ or 2 parts grit or fine chippings. Alternatively, use bracken litter or sedge peat in place of the leafmould, and high-quality light loam instead of the J.I. compost, ensuring that the loam is sterilized beforehand. Like the filling of any bed intended for a collection of plants, the latter is designed to be acceptable to the widest possible range of species. Where the bed is to be devoted to a limited and specialised collection, the soil mixture can be adjusted to suit more exact requirements.

Before filling the bed any large drainage holes should be covered with fine plastic mesh or perforated zinc and topped over with fine chippings. Firming of the soil mixture at several stages during the filling operation will minimize subsequent settlement and slumping, which can spoil the looks of the finished work; a good pressing down with the hands is sufficient, if done after each 8 cm (3 in) of filling. A soil mixture depth of 20 cm (8 in) is about the minimum required to meet the rooting needs of most cushion plants.

Then comes the most enjoyable part of the construction: the creation of a miniature terrain that holds a variety of planting places and aspects, and is pleasing to look at. Any attractive and shapely stones or rock fragments can be used, including tufa and 'manufactured' rocks made by moulding a mixture of coarse sand, cement and sieved peat (hyper-tufa). Lastly, of course, the whole surface has to be top-dressed with chippings, but before this is done any plants put by for the bed should be installed, it being much easier to do this before the covering of the soil mixture.

The same scheme can be carried out at ground level in the alpine house – well, almost – because a little elevation of the

bed is necessary to achieve the all-important drainage. This entails the building of a dwarf wall to raise the bed's surface about 15 cm (6 in) above the floor. The earth at ground level should be thoroughly forked over and loosened and then laced generously with grit before building begins. By so doing the effective depth of the bed is increased, and those plants that wish can root down into the extended root run. Very simple foundations are all that is necessary: just a thick layer of mortar on the firmed earth to take the first course of bricks, stones or blocks. From there on the soil mixture, filling, landscaping and planting are as already described. If larger rocks are placed at the rear of the bed, the surface can be sloped to make for easier maintenance and better display of the plants. This ground-level type is only suitable for houses with glass to the floor; solid-walled houses do not provide anything like enough light for the plants.

The upkeep and plant care required for these indoor gardens are very similar to those entailed in plunged pot culture in the alpine house, although the frequency of watering is less, particularly for the ground-based bed.

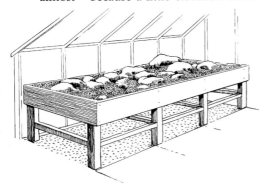

Fig. 19 A raised bed in an alpine house.

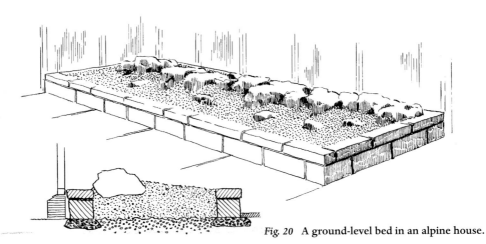

Fig. 20 A ground-level bed in an alpine house.

CHAPTER 5

Propagation

We do not propagate plants merely to produce replacements for those which are lost to disease, weather, pests or our own maltreatment; there are other good reasons for taking cuttings or sowing seed. Cuttings are the alternative when plants refuse to set seed or if seed becomes unavailable from the wild source; they are the primary means of sustaining and making available particular forms and clones. Seed gives us young plants free from inherited disease and can provide large numbers of plants from which we can select for colour, form, flowering and disease resistance. Seed is the usual means by which new species are introduced into cultivation.

TAKING CUTTINGS

Snipping off a shoot bearing several leaf-rosettes and using this as a cutting does not give a flying start to the achievement of a young plant; single rosettes produce the healthiest and most vigorous juveniles. The single rosette is on the current year's growth, with a youthful urge to develop, whereas larger multi-rosette cuttings have older stem material at the base, which is more reluctant to produce roots and if it does so, will have slow and less satisfactory growth. Unlike some other plant types cushions are not structured such that shoots may be plucked or levered away; they must be cleanly cut at their junction with the older stem. It does

not seem to matter which part of the cushion provides the cuttings, but generally those at the base of the mound are of greater length and hence easier to prepare and insert. Several weeks after the plant has finished flowering it is at its peak of root-forming activity, which means that its shoots are in the prime state for use as cuttings, being more disposed to form roots than at other times. At about four to six weeks after the last flowers have faded is the time when this optimum condition prevails.

Preparation

Most cuttings benefit from a little trimming and this is often a painstaking task. The purpose is to bare the lower part of the shoot by stripping off a few leaves, but they cannot be simply pulled away with tweezers; this tears the shoot tissue and discourages rooting as well as providing openings for the entry of disease. Each leaf must be cut close to the shoot's stem with a very sharp blade or scissors in excellent condition (Fig. 21). All dead and withered material should be included in the removal and any raggedness of the shoot base should be severed neatly. The very dense, minutely-leaved species do not permit such tidy preparation, nor the singling out of individual shoots, hence the best that can be done is to ensure that no dead material is left on the cutting (which may be a small cluster of rosettes).

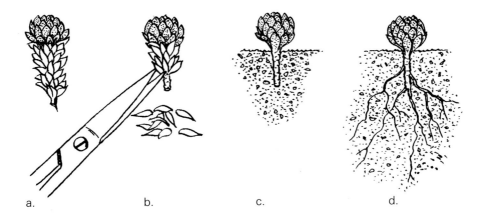

Fig. 21 Preparing a cutting: (a) typical single rosette cutting; (b) removal of withered leaves, and
trimming of stem; (c) insertion in sand; (d) cutting ready for potting.

The rooting medium

There have been quite a number of trials with new and promising materials possessing the essentials for a rooting medium, i.e. high water retention combined with a sharp granular structure, an abundance of tiny air spaces and freedom from fungus-carrying inclusions. Perlite, vermiculite and pumice have all produced acceptable results, but have not performed to an extent that makes them superior to coarse sand, still the most commonly-used rooting medium. Look for a sand which has a varied grain size, something like a mixture of refined white sugar and the coarser brown type. Sand with a noticeable dust content is unsuitable and the best way to check this is to dry out a sample and trickle it through the fingers. Also unsuitable are sands including tiny pebbles or coarse lentil-sized grains, and sands originating from calcareous rock.

Propagators

Mist units, bottom heat, rooting hormones and stem wounding are all aids or promoters for the formation of roots on cuttings, but for the great majority of cushion plants their use is unnecessary and largely ineffective. The methods in popular use and the equipment they require are simple and have yet to be convincingly improved upon.

The container for the sand may be a pot, a pan or a tray, but it should be non-porous; clay pots dry out far too quickly. The basic amateurs' type of propagator, comprised of a seed tray and a clear plastic cover, is totally adequate and even simpler units, contrived from pots or tubs and polythene bags, function reasonably well. In the matter of the container filling there is some contention; whilst most growers use only sand there are those who put a layer of compost below it. Advocates of the latter argue that cuttings can be left longer in the propagator as they are able to take up nutrients from the compost and build up a larger, stronger root system, but this reasoning falters when the two systems are compared. Where the filling is of sand only, the cutting is removed and potted as soon as it has enough root to cope with compost and gain benefit from it, hence in both cases it is provided with nutritious rooting when it is ready for it. There are in fact risks associated with the addition of compost in that moulds may start up if the compost has not been adequately sterilized and the cutting may become very drawn if its stay in the propagator is lengthened.

Treatment

It is often recommended that the cuttings be dunked in a fungicide solution just before insertion into the sand, yet there are equally good success rates where the grower relies upon the cuttings being clean and healthy and the equipment thoroughly sterilized, shunning fungicides altogether.

Ideally the rooting medium should be fully moist but not sodden, and if the sand has been well selected it is not difficult to achieve this state.

The tray, or other container, must have drainage holes in its base for the wetting method to succeed and if these allow the sand to trickle through, cover them with gauze or the glass fibre mat used in car repairs. By standing the container in water just deep enough to reach the base of the sand it will take up moisture by capillary action. When the sand surface shows the first signs of wetness the process is complete. A ten-minute drainage time is enough to let any excess run away and the sand is then ready for cutting insertion (Fig. 21).

Large fluctuations of temperature are detrimental to the raising of cuttings, hence the propagator should be situated in a place where conditions are as steady as possible, preferably sheltered from wind and rain and in good light, but not direct sun.

Rooting

For many cushion species a period of three to six weeks is sufficient for the formation of adequate roots. A rough guide to what constitutes 'adequate' is that there should be as least as much living material below the surface of the sand as above it (Fig. 21). To check root development

simply 'dig up' one or two of the cuttings using a small knife blade or suchlike and if they are not far enough advanced, gently replace and firm them in – no harm is done. For various reasons cuttings may take far longer to form roots. A few species are just naturally slow or difficult to strike, but often the delay is due to the time at which they were taken. Autumn, winter and early spring material can take many months to root, but circumstances may create the need to disregard the ideal. For instance, if a cherished plant is about to be lost or a fragment from a long-desired and precious species is offered, then whatever the time of year it is worth putting a few shoots in the propagator; there is nothing to lose and everything to gain.

It is not unusual for a cutting to become elongated (drawn) by the time it has made significant roots; in fact it can be a sign that the roots are growing. If the elongation has brought about a doubling or more of the shoot's original length then it is wise to snip off the top half; this will encourage branching and the subsequent development of compact growth.

Weaning

When the time comes to move the cutting out of the propagator a nursery compost should be prepared. This contains the ingredients suitable for the mature plant, but is refined by sieving out oversize material, such as large chippings and pellets of soil, peat or leafmould. The weaning pot need be no more than 7 cm (2½ in) in diameter and plastics are much the easier to manage, drying out less rapidly than clays, which must be plunged. The potted infants are kept in shade for at least a week and then, over the following few days, should be given increasing light until they are fully hardened and ready to enjoy adult conditions.

GROWING FROM SEED

There is always the possibility that something special may arise from the sowing of seed, whether it be from a garden source or a hitherto unexplored wild location. Chance adds zest to the work and the expectations, and those who become interested in seed raising learn to watch out for the unusual seedling, a variant that differs in rate of growth, colour, habit or other feature. Often it proves to be nothing but a runt in the litter or a rogue seed from some other plant, but just occasionally it can be an exceptional form or perhaps a beautiful and quite unexpected hybrid. Many of our highly valued plants have come to us in this manner.

When a batch of seed germinates well the amateur can be overwhelmed by success, having neither the need nor the accommodation for dozens of a single species. It is important to keep the seed-raising within manageable limits, resisting the temptation to acquire numerous packets and to sow every one of the seeds they contain.

Containers

The conventional seed tray is fine for the growers of bedding plants or vegetables, but is far too large for the pinch of seed which is likely to be the most that will be received by the cushion enthusiast. The sowing of several rows across a tray, one row for each species, produces problems later when germination is by no means simultaneous and some rows are ready for moving whilst others are just emerging or still to come. If small plastic pots are used, about 7 cm (2½ in) in diameter, each can be sown with a single species, thus avoiding the problems of irregular germination and also giving a greater depth of compost for the roots of the seedlings. The term 'seed pan', found frequently in rock gardening literature, is a relic from the times when nurserymen used large clay pans for their seed growing, quantity being no embarrassment.

Seed compost

Although there will be differences in the composts used for the various cushion types at a later stage, initially one compost is sufficient for all in their germination and early growth. It is more finely graded and, for some species, a little richer than that used beyond the seedling stage, and above all it must be clean, fresh and treated against infections. Good quality John Innes No. 1, passed through a 3 mm (⅛ in) sieve and mixed with an equal quantity of similarly-sieved clean grit, has all the properties required.

Sowing

After the compost has been lightly firmed in the pot its surface should be thinly but entirely covered with fine (3 mm) chippings, or alternatively, dust-free grit. The seed is sprinkled evenly over this surface. The pot is then watered by standing it, to about one-third of its depth, in clean water for a few minutes. Then comes the wait of several months, if the sowing has been made in late autumn or winter, as is usual. Much has been said in the past about the necessity for the seed of alpine plants to be frozen for a period, but this is now regarded as less important than was believed; nevertheless it can improve germination in some species. If the seed is stubborn or far from fresh when received, it may be a year or more before any germination occurs, hence keeping pots for two or three years can pay dividends. Seed obtained in spring should be sown promptly, but any arriving later is best held back until the growing season has ended, otherwise it may germinate with insufficient time remaining for the seedlings to gain enough strength and resistance to survive the approaching winter.

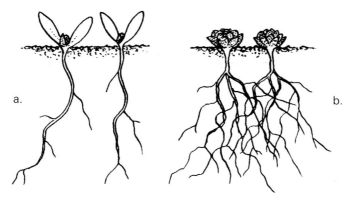

Fig. 22 Seedlings: (a) in early development and ready for potting; (b) more mature, with much larger and entangled root systems.

Treatment

Pampering the seed after sowing is, on the whole, ineffective. If it is going to germinate it will do so left open to the weather and there will be a natural culling out of the weaklings. The only precaution necessary is to protect the seed pots from very heavy rain, which can wash seeds away and batter newly germinated shoots into oblivion. The exceptions to this tough treatment are the choice species of *Dionysia* and *Raoulia*, which are rather frail when they first sprout and easily lost, so better kept under cover.

The transfer (pricking out) of a seedling to its nursery pot has a much less damaging and disrupting effect if it is done at an early state of growth. When the first true leaves begin to show between the cotyledon (Fig. 22) the root system is still simple and easily scooped out of the compost intact. Later, when the plantlet has developed a recognizable leaf-rosette, its roots have lengthened, wan-dered and intertwined with those of its neighbours and consequently some breakage and loss is inevitable in the move. The check suffered is greater and recovery takes longer.

The compost, potting and aftercare for seedlings are just the same as those for rooted cuttings.

OPPORTUNE PROPAGATION

Those cushions with a tendency to root down from their lowest shoots may provide offspring ready for immediate potting. A careful exploration can locate the points at which roots have developed and the shoots connected to these are then snipped clear and treated as rooted cuttings. Some species, particularly androsaces and drabas, produce self-sown young in the pots of mature plants. These are not difficult to winkle out when small and can be potted up like normal seedlings.

CHAPTER 6

Pests, diseases and other troubles

It might be said that the worst enemy of cushion plants is mould, and yet there are certain genera rarely affected by it. Aphids are a serious threat to some, but hardly ever found on others and slugs will crawl over one species to devour another. The one common destroyer is neglect, and much of the skill in keeping cushion plans healthy lies in the early recognition of trouble followed swiftly by effective treatment – but which treatment? The problems in caring for plants are akin to those of vetinary practice: our patients cannot tell us what is wrong and we can only strive to determine the cause from what we see and touch.

PESTS

Ants do not feed directly on plants, but their workings can cause extensive damage. In producing their labyrinths and nursery chambers beneath the ground they chop away any fine roots obstructing their paths and at the height of summer their spoil heaps can rise within the looser types of cushion, burying the foliage. This happens so frequently to certain *Dianthus* species that they must have some special attraction that draws the ants to build beneath them. Powder containing *Pyrethrum* toxin is sold in puffer packs for dusting the runs and nest entrances and there are poisoned baits in the form of a sweet syrup that are supposed to be carried back into the colony and put paid to all. The potency of these preparations can only be judged by results, and whilst the powder is quite effective, the syrup is unimpressive.

Aphids can be green, black, brown or white, but they are united in their concentration on sucking out the sap of living plants and breeding more aphids to suck more sap. The early stages of an aphid infestation can progress unnoticed in the congested foliage of a cushion plant and the first indication of their presence may not be a sight of the aphids themselves, but distress in the afflicted plant. The signs are a loss of tautness in the leaves, giving a generally flaccid look to the whole cushion and sometimes distortion of the leaf-rosettes and/or flowers. Yellowing of the leaves is another indicator, although this can also be a symptom of several other maladies. Added to the weakening effect of the attack is the threat of infection by disease carried in the piercing snouts of the pests and left to incubate unseen.

Those who abhor any use of chemical insecticides will be hard put to repel aphids from the multitude of nooks and crannies in a cushion. Attempts to remove them one by one with tweezers will probably injure the plant and also be never-ending. The employment of natural predators would require a small army of ladybirds or their larvae to achieve victory. Yet the concern over indiscriminate use of pesticides is, understandably, growing stronger every year and we growers must find means of using chemicals more safely in the protection of our plants and be alert to developments which might further reduce our dependence upon them.

Fortunately there is a very controlled and selective method available to us that is fully effective and no more expensive or troublesome to apply than those which are lethal to friend and foe alike. The systemic type of insecticide is absorbed through either the leaves or the roots and, without detriment to the health of the plant, is carried in its sap for several weeks. The only insects affected are those which actually feed on the sap of the plant. There are two methods by which these systemics can be applied: by spray or by take-up through the roots. In spraying there is a need to ensure that no beneficial creatures are on the plant at the time of treatment and that they are kept away until the foliage has dried. It should not be done in bright sunlight as this can cause damage to the plant. For the take-up method the maker's recommended dilution should be doubled to produce a half-strength mixture and applied in exactly the same manner as when watering the plant. Pot-grown specimens may be stood in a shallow container of the mixture for a few minutes. The great advantage of the take-up method is that no wetting of the cushion is involved. A further and valuable merit of systemic insecticide is its ability to affect root aphids, for they also succumb to the poison carried by the sap, especially if the take-up method is used.

If there is a misuse of systemics it is in the routine application practised by growers who are seemingly unable to tolerate even the possible presence of a single aphid in their treasured collections. To achieve this totality they dose all their plants at regular intervals to maintain the toxic level and so risk the very real danger of the enemy building up an immunity and also, perhaps, causing damage to the

plants in the long term. The responsible approach is, surely, to apply these useful substances with care and economy when they are needed and not on a 'just in case' basis.

There are also the so-called 'environment friendly' preparations, some of which are derived from plants possessing natural aphid toxins. *Pyrethrum* is one such plant, but its toxin only acts on contact and so has to be applied regularly, wetting the cushion each time. Sprays containing pirimicarb are marketed as harmless to bees, lacewings and ladybirds.

Caterpillars are obvious when they are grazing in broad daylight on fresh juicy leaves, but when the ravages of their eating are there to see and yet no caterpillars are to be found, we tend to assume that slugs must be to blame. This may be the case, unless the culprit is one of the nocturnal-feeding larvae of night moths. These caterpillars can be quite large, up to 4 cm (1½ in) long and are normally a drab yellow or brown in colour. They rest just beneath the soil surface during the day and are very good at lying concealed beneath the top-dressing of troughs and pots. The only really successful means of control is to hunt them after dark.

Nematodes are not normally listed as pests, but for the growers of cushion saxifrages the stem nematode can be a scourge. It is a microscopic, worm-like parasite that lives in the plant's tissues and there are no treatments available to the amateur for its control. So contagious is it that a knife used for taking cuttings can transfer infection from one plant to another, and it is also capable of migrating through moist soil to another host. The symptoms of its presence are distortions of the stems and flowers, stunted growth and progressive weakening of the plant. To confuse matters the early stages of these symptoms are very similar to the effects caused by a root fungus which can be controlled by the use of a systemic fungicide. Optimists should therefore treat suspected plants for the root fungus as a first step; then, if no improvement follows, assume the worst and destroy them. Unfortunately, because the flowering parts are the principal indicators, the test requires a whole year's waiting until the plants bloom again and during this time they should be quarantined to prevent possible further spreading of the blight.

Red spider mites are not true spiders, nor are they red, but are tiny, eight-legged bugs varying in colour from yellowish-green to ruddy brown. They can just about be seen with the (good) naked eye, but the more easily-noticed evidence of their presence is a grey-white mottling on leaves which develops into a fine webbing as the attack progresses. Yellowing and wilting of foliage signals serious infestation of these sap-suckers and the sad truth is that our defences against them are not very effective. The most successful deterrent is a cool, damp atmosphere, for the mites thrive in warm, dry environments. They have their natural predators, such as the anthocorids and the typhlodormids, some of which are now available to the amateur as predator packs for greenhouse use.

Chemical control is effective within limits and requires repeated application as the mite's eggs are unaffected. Systemics containing dimethoate or diazinon are the types used for control when the pest is at large and active in the summer.

Often mistaken for the mite and unjustly slaughtered is an innocent, pinhead-sized scarlet spider which dashes about in seemingly aimless circles on the sunny surfaces of paths and walls.

Slugs and snails are enemies in almost every branch of gardening and there is nothing that can be added to what has already been written and said, repeatedly,

concerning their habits and the means for their control.

Vine weevils look like small, brown-black beetles and have a very wide-ranging appetite. The adult will munch the leaves of anything from pot plants to large shrubs, but it is the larvae which wreak the greatest destruction. These are root-eating grubs, living permanently below ground, though they will partially surface, nocturnally, to gnaw at the bases of shoots. Strangely, there is no known male of the species, all adults being female and able to produce fertile eggs asexually. By the time that symptoms are apparent the damage may be terminal, as the grub's activities usually result in a sudden flagging of the plant victim, followed shortly by its death. Presumably the pest then pupates, having totally destroyed its own food supply. With a plentiful root mass to sustain it the grub has an active life of from 12 to 18 months prior to metamorphosis.

There has been a dramatic upsurge in vine weevil infestations over the past twenty years and it has coincided with a similarly rapid expansion in the use of peat-based composts. The experience of reputable growers supports the suspicion that the two are related.

Once arrived the vine weevil is virtually impossible to eradicate. The chemical which produced significant control has now been withdrawn and the substitutes perform poorly. The adults can be trapped in the same fashion as earwigs, by providing daytime hideaways of pots filled with straw or loosely rolled cardboard tubes which can be collected and their occupants destroyed. If it is suspected that a plant may be under attack it should be knocked out of its pot, or dug up and the grubs will be easily seen if they are present – comma-shaped, dull white and with a prominent brown head. To be sure that every one is detected and destroyed most of the soil or compost has to be removed from the root system; consequently the plant then needs to be nursed back into good health after replanting or repotting.

Recent work on appropriate predators has raised hopes that, at least for alpine house plants, a safe and efficient control may soon be available to us.

Woodlice are usually regarded as harmless scavengers, interested only in dead or dying vegetation, but the core of a cushion is made up almost entirely of dead leaves, and what is more it provides a hiding place that is warm, dark and protective. To the woodlouse a mature cushion plant is both larder and home, allowing it to live and multiply unseen until the damage that it is causing becomes apparent. As it browses on the withered foliage the insect severs the fine stems supplying the outer rosettes, which then die suddenly, puzzling the grower who can see no signs of disease. As woodlice do most of their eating and breeding in the warmer months it is in this period that the damage occurs and if rosettes begin to die off mysteriously the presence of lice should be suspected. The plucking out of affected rosettes sometimes disturbs and reveals the pests, but it may be necessary to pry into the heart of the cushion and beneath its base to find them. Once discovered they can be removed with tweezers; there is no need for chemical treatment.

Worms are so welcome in most parts of the garden that to include them as pests might seem odd, but in the confined space of a small trough, or worse still a pot, their tunneling and cast-making can be injurious to plants. The soil mounds which they excrete take valuable material away from roots and leave behind cavities; they also clog the surface dressing and, if piled over part of the cushion, set up rotting of the foliage. The only sure and harmless course of action is to find the worm and remove it. For troughs this requires a night patrol when the weather is moist and for the pot it means knocking out the plant and probing into the root ball. The latter action is severe and may result in the need for a complete repotting.

DISEASES

Moulds flourish where the atmosphere is humid and lifeless, when the summer weather turns sultry, when the autumn days are misty and still, when the cloud and drizzle of winter lasts for days. Their spores are invisible, but always present, waiting for favourable conditions and then growing rapidly wherever they find low resistance. Dead and dying vegetation offers them their starting points and as they progress and strengthen they increase their territory by infecting living tissue, causing it to wilt and weaken, creating more dying material upon which to grow further.

By its nature the cushion appears to be especially vulnerable to moulds, with the greater part of its mass composed of dead foliage, and the older it gets the larger is this proportion of susceptible material. Contrary to what might be expected, however, the onset of fungal infection usually begins not in the core of the cushion, but around the edges of the leaf-rosettes where the most recently withered leaves are located, and from there it moves inwards to their living centres. In species which are exceptionally prone to attack infection can begin almost anywhere, including the youngest of the leaves, which suggests that some weakening of the plant has already taken place due to a deficiency or a deterioration in conditions brought about by overwatering, humid air, excessive heat or similar problems of cultivation.

The earlier that a mould attack is recognized, the better are the prospects for successful treatment. First aid begins with the removal of all the obviously affected material and any that is suspect. With some cushions it is possible to pluck out afflicted rosettes using tweezers, but there is always the risk that healthy growth may be dragged out with the bad. The more painstaking but safer method is carefully to trace back each mould-affected shoot to where it branches from sound growth and to sever it at that point using a scalpel (or similar razor-sharp blade) or fine scissors.

After the removal operation, neighbouring rosettes can be gently rearranged to fill the cavity.

The next step is to aid the plant in resisting further attack by applying a systemic fungicide. Outdoor plants are easy to treat using a fine spray, but very sensitive and difficult species living in the alpine house may resent even the briefest wetting of their cushions by spray, and the fungicide must be applied by take-up through the root system. For this the pots stand in a shallow bath of a half-strength solution, with great care taken to avoid over-wetting the compost. With a solution depth of not more than 2 or 3 cm (1 in) the soak time should not exceed 3 to 4 minutes. Systemic fungicides may cause

Fig. 23 Removal of afflicted rosettes, using a slim spatula and scissors.

physical damage to plants if they are applied by spray to subjects in strong sunlight.

The labour and effects of any treatment may be wasted if no attempt is made to determine and correct (if possible) whatever it is that has encouraged the fungal attack. Checks should be made on ventilation, drainage, compost and plunge moistness, and so on.

The application of systemic fungicides is open to the same abuses as their insecticide counerparts. Those growers who maintain round-the-year routine applications in an attempt to render their plants 'mould-proof' are ignoring or unaware of the risk that immune strains of fungus may develop, with all the horrors that this would bring. A traditional defence against winter moulds is the dusting of the plants with sulphur powder. The effect is rather unsightly; however, it can stave off mild attacks and at least acts as a deterrent, but it is not effective as a cure when the disease has obtained a hold.

Virus diseases are complex and as far as the amateur is concerned extremely difficult to diagnose and impossible to cure. Lack of vigour is the most obvious symptom, but then so it is for several other ills. If virus is suspected the plant(s) concerned should be destroyed, preferably by burning, as the disease can be transmitted all too easily.

OTHER TROUBLES

Bird damage: As though on a sudden impulse, certain birds will sometimes attack cushions that they have completely ignored for months or even years. Blackbirds are the chief culprits, but sparrows and starlings will also have a go if the mood takes them. Why they do it is puzzling, for they do not take away the rosettes that they pluck out, but fling them around in the vicinity of the target plant. It can hardly be that they are searching for aphids, but spiders, grubs and other sundry bugs may be hidden in the dense foliage, and maybe these are the attraction. On the other hand the behaviour might be another form of the mysterious compunction that causes yellow crocus flowers to be savaged (in some gardens) by flocks of avian vandals.

Plastic netting, of the type used for fruit cages, is easily fixed to light wooden frames for fitting over plunge beds, and will give full protection, but in the garden such defence is impractical and an eyesore. For individual plants in beds, florist's wire, which is soft iron and sold in bundles of just the right length, is a very effective deterrent. A few lengths pushed into the soil for about half their length, and spaced a hand's-span apart, will scare off birds without harming them; and cats too. This method should be used with caution, however, for the fine and almost invisible wires pose a threat of eye damage to the young or the incautious.

Bleached leaves may be a symptom of virus infection, but when these appear early in the year the cause might be less sinister. A mild spell in late winter can bring about premature germination of seeds or growth of new shoots and it is these that are prone to the effect, the young leaves being a creamy-white instead of a healthy fresh green. However, with the increase in day length and a strengthening of light, the pallid leaves may well colour up and grow on normally, hence it seems reasonable to assume that light deficiency is responsible for the condition in such cases. It is a matter of 'wait and see'. If there is no improvement after five or six weeks then virus may be the culprit and the affected plants should be destroyed.

Die-back is most prevalent in the Hima-layan species and occurs during the dormant period, for no apparent reason. It may affect one or two rosettes or a considerable part of the cushion and, occasionally, the whole plant. The first sign is a wilting and dulling of the leaf-rosette(s), followed by a speedy progression through yellowing and browning, to death, within a few days. Where it is localized the injury may or may not spread to the remaining healthy foliage. If its onset is noticed very early it is sometimes possible to save the afflicted shoots by snipping them out and treating them as cuttings, when they may recover and make roots to become unblemished young plants. This strange behaviour suggests that the cause is not a disease, but a breakdown of supply in the plant's system. It is possible that inadequate moisture at the root may be a strong contributory factor, producing what might be termed a 'winter drought'. Similar symptoms can also result, however, from the activities of soil pests such as root aphids, vine weevil and other larvae, and a check for these should be made before attributing the losses to this puzzling phenomenon.

Scorch is the word used by rock gardeners to describe the browning and withering of leaf-rosettes on cushions and it is attributed to excessive exposure to the sun. It is hard to accept that those plants accustomed to the intense sunlight of Alpine heights could be distressed by the heavily-filtered light that reaches our lowland gardens. A more probable cause is the overstressing of the plant's system when the roots are unable to provide moisture quickly enough to the transpiring leaves. In response the plant abandons the worst-affected foliage, starting with that most exposed to the sun – which is invariably where scorch begins. The result can be a cushion with its south side browned to a crisp, its east and west flanks yellowed and a healthy green on the north side. Underwatering may be the cause of such damage, but another may be that the cultivated plant rarely has a depth or spread of root system comparable to that in nature and is consequently more quickly and easily stressed. A further possibility is the loss of roots from the depredations of soil pests: unnoticed when water supplies are generous, but crippling when these are reduced.

Tall cushions are not common, but where they do occur the deformity affects many rather than one or two in a collection. The domes of St Paul's in London and St Peter's in Rome were designed with great artistry to satisfy the eye, but a similarly-shaped cushion has none of their appeal, probably because we know that it should not be that way. Inadequate side-lighting causes an upward drawing of growth and solid-walled frames will often produce this distortion, as will plunge beds with sides which tower above the surface of the sand filling.

Quick reference plant list

The purpose of this list is to present the reader with brief details for each of the plants described in the body of the book. It is intended for use in conjunction with plant catalogues and seed lists, or for any other occasion when all that is required is a sketch of the plant, i.e. its natural habit, appearance and cultural needs. The remarks regarding cultivation concentrate on the treatment which has, in general, produced the best results under British conditions. It is accepted that most of the plants can be grown as alpine house subjects, but where, in individual cases, life under glass can actually be detrimental, this is advised. As a key to the abbreviated cultural comments the following is offered:

Open garden is applied to plants suitable for the conventional rock garden, with the assumption that some attempt has been made to provide good light, drainage and an appropriate soil mixture; also that no form of weather protection is used.

Trough or bed embraces the many forms of trough and specially-built, raised containments, filled with carefully prepared soil mixtures, and which may have partial or full winter cover.

Plunge refers to pot-grown plants held in one of the various types of outdoor plunge bed, equipped with the means for overhead protection.

Alpine house is reserved for those species which are best kept as full-time residents of the alpine house, or in permanently-covered plunge beds.

Omitted from the list are those species and hybrids given only passing reference in the main text, and also species only recently brought into cultivation, which have still to be fully evaluated, and in any case are already only briefly described for want of more knowledge and experience in their culture.

Acantholimon venustum

From high ridges of calcareous rock. A fairly quick-growing hummock of spiny leaves, with wands of pink bloom. Open garden, trough or bed in full sun. (p. 73)

Androsace alpina

Of acid rocks and stony wastes, forming a low cushion with sessile flowers in shades of rose. Trough, bed or plunge, with maximum light. Not for the alpine house. (p. 14)

A. brevis

A crevice and stony ground dweller in non-calcareous formations. Low cushion with rich pink flowers. Slow-growing and short-lived (in cultivation). Trough or bed in full light. Resents alpine house culture. (p. 15)

A. carnea

Grows in short turf on non-calcareous ground. Umbels of pink flowers on medium stems above dark-green foliage. An easy species for open garden, trough or bed. (p. 15)

A. carnea x pyrenaica

Usually makes a good cushion, but variable in flower, from pink to white, on short stems or sessile. Trough or bed. (p. 24)

A. ciliata

From acid and calcareous screes and rocks. A strong grower with short-stemmed, deep-pink blooms. Trough, bed or plunge, with good light and winter cover. (p. 16)

A. cylindrica

Crevice plant of limestone cliffs. Fairly strong in growth, with generous white flowers on short stems. Plunge with winter cover. Shade lightly from hottest sun. (p. 17)

A. cylindrica x hirtella

A willing hybrid with a well-mounded cushion and plentiful, sessile, white flowers. Trough, bed or plunge, with winter cover. (p. 24)

A. delavayi

From high-altitude screes of non-calcareous rock. Scented, white, sessile flowers on a smooth, light-green cushion. Trough, bed or plunge, in full light, with winter cover. (p. 18)

A. globifera

A vigorous species from slopes of short turf on acid rock. Sessile, lilac flowers. Trough or bed, with winter cover and full light. (p. 18)

A. hausmannii

Small, short-lived crevice-dweller of limestone cliffs. Grey-green rosettes ringed with very short-stemmed white flowers. Trough, bed or plunge, with good light and winter cover. (p. 19)

A. hedraeantha

From turfed and stony slopes in regions of acidic schists and volcanic rock. Very like *A. carnea* in appearance; flowers pink and occasionally white. Trough or bed. (p. 19)

A. helvetica

A high-altitude crevice species of limestone and, occasionally, acid formations. Grey-green dense cushion, liberally covered in sessile white flowers. Best suited to the alpine house all year round. (p. 19)

A. hirtella

Of limestone cliff habitats, with grey-green foliage and white scented flowers on very short stems, generously produced. Plunge or alpine house. (p. 20)

A. × marpensis

Hybrid of *A. globifera* and *A. muscoidea longiscapa*. Vigorous grower, with sessile, lilac flowers. Bed or plunge. Winter cover. (p. 24)

A. muscoidea

Tightly clustered, hairy rosettes. The 'Schacht form' has single, white, sessile flowers. The *longiscapa* form bears multiple heads, lilac to deep pink. Trough or bed with winter cover. (p. 20)

A. pubescens

From calcareous and acid rocks – rare. A dense, grey-green cushion, with white, sessile flowers. Plunge or alpine house. (p. 21)

A. pyrenaica

A crevice-dweller from granite cliffs. Dark-green, tiny-leaved rosettes and almost sessile, white flowers in profusion. Plunge or alpine house. Shade from hottest sun. (p. 21)

A. vandellii

Another granite crevice species, with a perfect cushion of silver-grey and incomparable massed flowers of pure white. Definitely for the alpine house. (p. 22)

Arabis androsacea

A grey, furry little bun that grows slowly. White, cruciform flowers on small scapes. Alpine house culture. (p. 74)

Asyneuma pulvinatum

From crevices in limestone cliffs and rocks. A neat cushion, with tiny campanulate flowers of blue or lilac. Full light. Alpine house. (p. 74)

Bolax gummifera

A soft but dense mound of exquisite foliage, each leaf silvered around its edges. Trough or bed. (p. 75)

Celmisia argentea

From slopes comprised mainly of shattered, acid rock, and subject to frequent rainfall. A neat mound of stiff, silvery rosettes, with white 'daisies'. Trough, bed or plunge, with winter cover if found necessary. (p. 76)

C. sessiliflora

Habitat similar to *C. argentea*. Makes a fine silver dome, and flowers white at foliage level. Trough, bed or plunge. Winter cover. (p. 76)

Crassula sediformis

A tightly-massed mound of bright-green leaf-rosettes of succulent character. Umbels of numerous, tiny white flowers. Open garden. (p. 76)

Dianthus alpinus

From thin turf and stony ground in limestone areas. A hump of dark-green, glossy leaf-rosettes bearing huge flowers of white, pink or burgundy. Open garden, trough or bed. (p. 26)

D. erinaceus

Can make great mounds of its spiny, close foliage, and flowers rather sparingly with pink, fringed blooms. Open garden, with maximum sun. (p. 27)

D. freynii

Grows in short turf on sunny slopes in limestone hills. Slowly makes a rounded, grassy cushion, and provides many white or pink flowers. Trough or bed. (p. 27)

D. haematocalyx

From limestone peaks and ridges. A neat, blue-green tuffet, with burgundy flowers, and a tawny reverse to their petals. Trough or bed. (p. 28)

D. microlepis

A tight, dwarf cushion bearing sessile flowers in a range of rose to magenta. From acid rocks and stone piles. Trough or bed in full light. (p. 28)

D. pavonius (syn. D. neglectus)

From several locations in the Alps, the best forms being at high levels on non-calcareous, stony ground. A neat, grassy-leaved mound, with rose-pink flowers. Trough or bed in full light.(p. 30)

Dionysia afghanica

A firm, mounded cushion, with open rosettes of faintly veined leaves and closely held flowers of pale lilac, enhanced by a darker eye. Alpine house only. (p. 34)

D. archibaldii

A slightly loose cushion, flowering modestly with golden-eyed, light violet blooms, very early in the year. Alpine house only. (p. 35)

D. aretioides

The easiest of the cushion dionysias. Robust quick-growing cushions, smothered in flowers of pale to deep, golden yellow. Usually an alpine house subject, but can be grown in trough or bed with winter cover. (p. 35)

D. bryoides

A tiny-leaved hard cushion with a great zest for all-over blooming from an early age. Pink, clear-eyed flowers and greyish-green leaves. Alpine house only. (p. 36)

D. curviflora

Makes a low mound of small, congested leaf-rosettes, and in the good forms blooms fairly generously, with pink to carmine flowers. Unusual in its requirement for a non-limy compost. Alpine house only. (p. 36)

D. diapensifolia

A very difficult species in cultivation. Makes a tidy, small bun of grey-green leaves, and flowers golden yellow from a very early age. Alpine house only. (p. 43)

D. freitagii

Slightly sticky, prominently-veined leaves form open rosettes in a firm well-shaped cushion. Sessile flowers of mauve with a yellow eye. Alpine house only. (p. 38)

D. involucrata

One of the easier species, and unusual in its flowering with raised umbels of lilac/magenta. Normally an alpine house subject, but can be grown in troughs or beds with winter cover. (p. 39)

D. janthina

Very similar to D. curviflora, but a limestone plant. Flowers in late autumn/winter. An alpine house subject, difficult to maintain. (p. 39)

D. lamingtonii

Makes a golden disc of crowded flowers in early spring. A very tight, firm, low cushion. Alpine house only. (p. 40)

D. michauxii

A difficult but very rewarding species. The growth is dense and grey-green. Golden-yellow flowers, can be numerous in well-kept specimens. Alpine house only. (p. 41)

D. tapetodes

Precise and strong-growing, in farinose and non-farinose forms. Plentiful immaculate yellow flowers. Among the easier species in cultivation, but still best as an alpine house resident. (p. 41)

Note: Unless stated otherwise, all the dionysias listed are from limestone habitats and seek a measure of shade from direct sun.

Diosphaera asperuloides (syn. Trachelium asperuloides)

A soft, pale green tuffet, covered in high summer with powder-blue starry flowers. From limestone habitats. Best suited to alpine house culture. (p. 77)

Draba acaulis

An extremely hairy, crouched hump of grey-green leaf-rosettes. Flowers almost sessile, in a golden yellow. From high limestone cliffs. Best in alpine house. (p. 45)

D. bryoides

Moss-like, green bun of congested leaf-rosettes. Flowers yellow on short stalks. From stony slopes on calcareous formations. Trough, bed or tufa, with winter cover if needed. (p. 46)

D. dedeana

From crevices in high-level limestones. A dark-green, bristly hump, with numerous papery white flowers. Trough, bed or plunge, with winter cover. (p. 46)

D. longisiliqua

A soft, grey-green cushion from hot lime-stone cliffs. Grows quickly, and flowers on long, wiry stalks with heads of clear yellow. Alpine house. (p. 47)

D. mollissima

A downy green mound of small, crowded rosettes, bearing a swarm of lemon-yellow flowers. From cliff and rock crevices. Best in the alpine house. (p. 47)

D. polytricha
Very similar in foliage and form to the above, but flowering bright-yellow on slender, whippy stalks. Alpine house. (p. 47)

D. rigida
A totally hardy and long-lived species, with a bright-green cushion of tiny, narrow leaves, and golden flowers on wiry stalks. Open garden, trough or bed. (p. 48)

Edraianthus pumilio
From limestone rocks on summit ridges. A grassy-leaved, grey-green tuffet, with large bell-flowers of lavender blue. Trough or bed in full sun. (p. 78)

Eriogonum shockleyi
From hot, dry, stony slopes. A silver-leaved low dome, bearing round heads of pale yellow or cream bloom. Alpine house. (p. 79)

Eritrichium nanum
A high-altitude crevice plant, forming a pewter-green hairy mound, spangled with intense blue 'forget-me-not' flowers. Very difficult, and for the alpine house. (p. 80)

Gypsophila aretioides
An extremely dense, hard cushion, from exposed calcareous rocks. Dark green, minute leaves and sparse white starry flowers. Trough or bed. (p. 80)

Haastia pulvinaris
An intensely woolly mound of congested rosettes. The finest of the New Zealand 'Vegetable Sheep', from bleak, rocky slopes of acidic formations. Trough, bed or plunge, with winter cover. (p. 81)

Helichrysum pagophyllum
An easy silver-leaved cushion grown mainly for foliage effect. Open garden, trough or bed. (p. 82)

H. sessiloides (syn. H. sessile)
From basalt cliffs and screes. A srongly consti-tuted species, with silver-green foliage and white 'everlasting flowers'. Open garden trough or bed, with winter cover. (p. 82)

Kelseya uniflora
A very dwarf conjested shrub, from exposed lime-stone cliffs and a harsh climate. Tiny white-pink blossoms, completely sessile. Best suited to alpine house culture. (p. 83)

Myosotis pulvinaris
Makes a dense, huddled bun of hairy, grey-green leaves, and flowers with white, sessile 'forget-me-

nots'. From high, stony slopes. Safest in the alpine house. (p. 85)

M. uniflora
A plant of unstable shingles at lower levels. Flowers yellow over a dark green, loose cushion. Best suited to the covered plunge or alpine house. (p. 85)

Nassauvia gaudichaudii
From poor, acidic, sandy soils in the Falkland Islands. Spiny, dark green leaves and oddly-petalled cream flowers. Open garden, trough or bed. (p. 86)

Petrocallis pyrenaica
From limestone screes and stony slopes. Pale lilac cruciform flowers sit close on a low-growing cushion of bright green foliage. Trough or bed, with winter cover for best results. (p. 87)

Primula allionii
A crevice-dweller of soft limestone cliffs. Forms a compact mound of large, sticky leaves, and flowers profusely, in a range from white through pink to carmine. Covered plunge or alpine house, with some shade. (p. 90)

Pygmaea pulvinaris
From wet mountain flanks in regions of acid rock. An almost moss-like cushion of dark green, minute leaves, and sessile, white flowers sparsely produced in cultivation. Trough or bed, with winter cover. (p. 91)

Raoulia bryoides
Neat and small rosettes, with a flannel-like surface, form a well-rounded dome of pale grey. Flowers rarely if ever set in cultivation. Trough, bed or plunge, with winter cover. (p. 51)

R. buchananii
The tightest possible arrangement of leaf-rosettes. Abundant, small silvery hairs give a sheen to the immaculate dome. Flowers insiginifant (in culti-vation). Plunge, with winter cover. (p. 52)

R. eximea
A silvery-green, extremely dense cushion of 'honeycomb' rosettes. One of New Zealand's 'Vegetable Sheep'. Flowers insignificant (in cultivation) Plunge, with winter cover. (p. 53)

R. mammilaris
A slow-growing, solid dome of tiny, fluffy leaf-rosettes, appearing almost white. A difficult and usually short-lived species in cultivation. Plunge with winter cover. (p. 54)

R. rubra

Very similar in all respects to *R. buchananii* and responding to the same culture. Not easy to obtain. (p. 55)

Note: All the species of *Raoulia* listed above are from exposed, rocky habitats, and root into non-calcareous material.

Sagina boydii

A British native, found in gritty, acid ground. Grown for its unique, very dark green and shiny cushion. Trough or bed. (p. 92)

Saxifraga burseriana

From limestone rocks and debris. Huge, white flowers on reddish stems, crowded over a spiny, silver-leaved mass of rosettes. Trough, bed or plunge, with winter cover for best results. (p. 57)

S. caesia

A crevice plant of sunny limestone rocks and cliffs. Cupped white flowers, on slender stems. Small, heavily encrusted leaves, and very tight growth. Trough or bed in full sun. (p. 58)

S. callosa

From sunny and semi-shaded cliffs of limestone, at low altitudes. A vigorous and variable 'silver' type with plumes of white bloom. Open garden or trough. (p. 64)

S. cebennensis

A tightly-growing 'mossy' type. Soft, green foliage, and a wealth of white flowers on slim stems. Trough or bed in partial shade. A plant of limestone gorges. (p. 67)

S. exarata

A 'mossy' from a wide range of locations, in several types of rock. Very varied in form and flower colour (white/yellow/pink). Trough, bed or plunge. (p. 67)

S. ferdinandi-coburgi

From limestone clefts and rocks. A kabschia type, with a hearty constitution. Golden flowers massed over a hard, smooth cushion. Trough or bed. (p. 59)

S. georgei

One of the Himalayan miniature kabschias. A moss-like mound, set with pure white, sessile flowers. Trough, bed or plunge, with winter cover. (p. 60)

S. lilacina

Another Himalayan, with a dislike of limy soils. Soft lilac blooms on short stalks, above a hard dark green mound. Trough, bed or plunge, with some shade. (p. 61)

S. marginata

From many limestone mountains in Europe. An easy and rewarding species, with a silvery-grey, low cushion and numerous milk-white flowers. Open garden, trough or bed. (p. 61)

S. oppositifolia ssp. rudolphiana

Makes a rounded, minutely-leaved bun, and puts up relatively giant, sessile flowers of deep rosy-purple. Of crevices in softer schists. Trough, bed or plunge, with peaty soil and partial shade. (p. 92)

S. paniculata

Very widespread, with a strong preference for acidic rock formations. Large, encrusted rosettes, and panicles of white or rose flowers. Open garden. (p. 65)

S. pedemontana

From lightly shaded granite rocks and debris. Makes a soft dome of downy foliage, and flowers with goblets of pearl-white to hide the cushion. Best treated as an alpine house or covered plunge subject. (p. 68)

S. pubescens

A high alpine species from acid schists. 'Mossy'-type foliage and form, but tighter. Almost sessile white flowers. Best suited to alpine house, or plunge bed with winter cover. (p. 69)

S. scardica

A kabschia type, from limestone rocks and screes. Leaf rosettes like tiny silver-grey pineapple tufts. Large flowers on substantial stems. Trough or bed, with mid-day shade. (p. 62)

S. valdensis

The dwarf of the 'silver' types. Native to hot and exposed rocks. Makes an incredibly compressed, warty mound, and flowers white on short scapes. Plunge or alpine house. (p. 66)

Silene acaulis

A crevice and scree plant, found on both acid and calcareous formations. Long-lived, sturdy hummocks of narrow-leaved rosettes, covered in pink to deep rose stemless campion flowers. Trough, or bed, but best in tufa. Full light. (p. 94)

Sources for plants and seeds

NURSERIES

Some of the larger garden centres have quite comprehensive 'Alpines' sections, in which a few cushion species are included, but on the whole it is the small specialist nurseries where the best of the cushions are to be found. But even there the stocks of the very choice species may be so small that they are not listed in the catalogues, and it becomes a matter of writing or 'phoning around to seek them out. The proprietors of these valuable sources are often devoted growers with an expert knowledge of their plants, and will gladly offer detailed advice on cultivation and care; they are frequently involved in the introduction of new and rare species through association with expeditions and have extensive contacts in the world of plants.

The nurseries listed here are selected from those which are well established and frequented by rock gardeners, but new ones are regularly coming into being and should not be overlooked in any search for cushion plants.

England

R. F. Beeston
294 Ombersley Road
Worcester
WR3 7HD

Graham's Hardy Plants
(G. E. Nicholls)
'Southcroft'
North Road
Timsbury
Bath
BA3 1JN

Hartside Nursery
Garden
nr Alston
Cumbria
CA9 3BL

Highgates Alpines (R.
E. & D. I. Straughan)
166A Crich Lane
Belper
Derbyshire
DE56 1EP

W. E. Th. Ingwerson
Ltd
Birch Farm Nursery
Gravetye
East Grinstead
W. Sussex
RH19 4LE

L. Kreeger
91 Newton Road
Ashtead
Surrey
KT21 1NN.

Potterton & Martin
The Cottage Nursery
Moortown Road
Nettleton
nr Caistor
Lincolnshire
LN7 6HX

Waterperry
Horticultural Centre
Alpine Dept
nr Wheatley
Oxfordshire
OX9 1LJ
(*Specializing in
saxifrages*)

Scotland

Ardfearn Nursery (J. &
A. Sutherland)
Bunchrew
Inverness
IV3 6RH

Craig Lodge Nurseries
Balmaclellan
Castle Douglas
Kirkubrightshire
DG7 3QR

Jack Drake
Inshriach Alpine Plant
Nursery
Aviemore
Invernessshire
PH22 1QS

Edrom Nurseries (J.
Jermyn)
Coldingham
Eyemouth
Berwickshire
TD14 5TZ

Christie's Nursery
'Downfield'
Main Road
West Muir
Kirriemuir
Angus
DD8 5LP

Wales

Aberconwy Nursery
Graig
Glan Conwy
Gwynedd
LL28 7TL

Northern Ireland

Timpany Nurseries
(Susan Tindall)
Margharetimpany
Road
Ballynahinch
Co. Down.

United States

Colorado Alpines, Inc.
P.O. Box 2708
Avon
CA 81620

Mt Tahoma Nursery
Rick Lupp
28111 12th Avenue E.
Graham
Washington 98338

Siskiyou Rare Plant
Nursery
2825 Cummings Road
Medford
OR 9750

SEED

The Alpine Garden Society and the Scottish Rock Garden Club operate similar seed exchange schemes, whereby mem-bers can obtain a quota, of their own selection, for a very modest price. The seed is donated by gardeners, botanical organisations and collectors in the field, from many parts of the world. Other societies and clubs operate similar systems. Sources for the newer and rarer are generally the expeditions that carry out authorized collecting in the wild. Shares are offered by the organisers and the shareholders enjoy the pick of the harvest when it is brought back.

Commercial suppliers of seed advertise in the various rock gardening journals and the horticultural press. These can be nurseries, seedsmen or just individual retailers. The following list is a selection and by no means exhaustive.

Wales

J. & J. Archibald
'Bryn Collen'
Ffostrasol
Llandysul
Dyfed
SA44 5SN

England

C. Chadwell
81 Parlaunt Road
Slough
Berkshire
SL3 8BE

Chiltern Seeds
Bortree Style
Ulverston
Cumbria
LA12 7PB

L. Kreeger
91 Newton Wood
Road
Ashtead
Surrey
KT21 1NN

Southern Hemisphere
Seed
17 Newton Avenue
Newton Hill
Wakefield
WF1 2PX

New Zealand

Southern Seeds
The Vicarage
Sheffield 8173

United States

Alplains
32315 Pine Crest court
Kiowa
CO 80117

Northwest Native Seed
Ron Ratko
915 Davis Place South
Seattle
WA 98144

Rocky Mountain Rare
Plants
P.O. Box 200483
Denver
CO 80220

Southwestern Native
Seeds
Box 50503
Tucson
AZ 85703

Note:

As the need for conservation becomes ever more apparent there is a growing awareness of the fragile hold on existence that some plants have in their native habitats, particularly amongst those in harsh environments. Several countries have now banned any collection of seed (or plants) by unauthorized groups or individuals. It as well to bear this in mind whilst holidaying abroad, and to make careful enquiries beforehand.

Choosing and buying plants

Nurseries vary in the ways that they rear, grow on and present their plants for sale. They compete in a commercial world and, as in any other business, are obliged at least to consider such things as achieving the end product in less time and at less cost, making economies by reducing the range and diversity of the product, using cheaper materials and processes, and so on. Good nurseries will make sensible savings where they can and adopt new technologies and goods where these will help in reducing labour and costs, but they will draw the line at anything which dilutes the quality and character of their plants. The methods and materials used in rearing a young plant can affect its subsequent behaviour and the ease, or otherwise, with which it can be introduced into its new, permanent home. Bad nursery practices are not always apparent, but there are checks that ought to be made when making a direct purchase, both as to the general quality of the stock and in the choice of one particular plant from a batch.

SIZE

Where there is variation of size in the plants the temptation is to pick the biggest, on the basis of value for money, or perhaps on the assumption that the larger the plant the more healthy and well found it must be. This is sometimes so, but examine it first; it may be a left-over from the previous year's stock, with a congested root mass within the pot that will be impossible to loosen without considerable damage, yet if left as it is may never develop a good root system when it is planted out or put into its new pot. Merely lifting the pot may reveal that the roots are through the drainage holes and into the grit or sand beneath. If such is the case it is an obvious reject, but look also for a mat of roots at the surface of the compost which is also a sign that the plant may be pot-bound. Smaller specimens are likely to have a freer root system, which is easily teased out to promote its future spread. With their youthful vigour small plants often overtake those of older stock and settle in their new homes more quickly. Check, if possible, whether the compost is peat-based or soil-based, and if the former, then try for the same plant where soil-based mixtures are used; if none can be had buy the smallest (healthy) specimen, in the hope that it has not had too long to become accustomed to its ball of peat and nutrients, and can be persuaded to accept a leaner, more natural root run for the rest of its life.

CONDITION

A plant that is pallid when compared to the others around it may be pot-bound, virus infected or a victim of aphids or vine weevil, and should be left where it is. Where a cushion shows limpness in its foliage, or has a dull appearance, it may only be in need of water, but there might be weevil grubs gnawing at its roots or aphids sucking the sap from them, and it should be passed by. Cushions with gaps in the foliage showing old and woody stems beneath are probably pot-bound and lacking nutrients, having exhausted the compost. Plants in this condition are unlikely to recover fully when replanted and hence will never make good specimens. Any cushion with dead rosettes in its make-up, or cavities where such have been plucked out, shows lack of care by the nursery; it may recover and heal its wounds, but there is a risk and it is best avoided.

CHARACTER

The great advantage to selecting a plant from a group in the nursery frame, or on the stall, is the opportunity to acquire a 'good form'. If the plants have been raised from cuttings taken from a solitary stock plant then the variation will be negligible, but seed-raised plants will often have slight individual differences, such as colour or wealth of flower, compactness of growth, leaf form, hairiness, and the buyer can choose those characteristics that he or she favours. On a juvenile plant unusually large flowers can cause it to stand out amongst its fellows, yet it may not make the best mature plant; others with smaller blooms can ultimately produce closer coverage of their cushions and present a more refined appearance. Seedlings or rooted cuttings which outpace the rate of growth for the great majority of the batch are rarely destined to be the best performers at the time of flowering; sometimes the smaller-leaved, compact and slow-growing youngsters become the choice forms in adulthood.

PLANTS BY POST

The number of nurseries no longer offering a postal service is continually increasing, the cost of packaging and postage being now so high that the bill for small and even medium-sized orders far exceeds the total price for the plants. Another draw-back is the behaviour of gritty composts *en route*, which despite the best efforts of the packer may not all stay in the pots, and a sorry bundle is finally delivered to the none-too-pleased purchaser. Nurseries prepared to send plants overseas are even fewer since phyto-sanitary controls were tightened and costly certification is now involved.

DEFECTIVE PLANTS

Most nurseries try very hard to provide plants which are free from pests or diseases, but these can lurk unsuspected before the plant's condition betrays their presence. If, when the purchased plant is brought home and taken from its pot, pests such as vine weevil grubs or root aphids are discovered, don't tell your friends, tell the nursery. If it is one of good repute the proprietors will be grateful for your warning. The plant may be a single victim, but the nursery needs to know about the infestation so that checks of the stocks can be made and any action swiftly taken. You will doubtless be offered, at least, a healthy replacement, together with their thanks for your discretion.

THIRSTY TRAVELLERS

Clay pots are still used by some nurserymen, especially for choice and difficult subjects. They are invariably set in plunge to conserve moisture levels by retarding evaporation, but as soon as they are lifted out the drying rate increases dramatically. The buyer may have a drive of several hours for the journey home, lengthened perhaps by a stop for a meal or a visit to friends. If the day is warm the little clays in the car can suffer accelerated drying, to the extent that by the time the plants receive attention they may be permanently damaged by dehydration, or even beyond recovery. It is safer to have a watering halt than to assume that the plants were moist enough to sustain them when purchased.

Clubs and societies

There are two organizations in Britain which are concerned exclusively with the cultivation and study of alpine/rock garden plants: The Alpine Garden Society and The Scottish Rock Garden Club. Both produce regular publications dealing with a wide range of related topics and hold shows in many parts of the country. They also operate very comprehensive seed exchange systems for the benefit of their members. Other countries have comparable bodies, for example: The North American Rock Garden Society, The New Zealand Alpine Garden Society, The Alpine Club of British Columbia and The Japanese Alpine Garden Society.

United Kingdom

The Secretary,
Mr E. M. Upward,
The Alpine Garden
  Society
A. G. S. Centre
Avon Bank
Pershore
Worcestershire
WR10 2JP

Membership Secretary,
Mrs J. Thomlinson
Scottish Rock Garden
  Club
1 Hillcrest Road
Bearsden
Glasgow
G61 2EB

North America

North American Rock
  Garden Society
Jacques Mommens,
Executive Secretary
P. O. Box 67
Millwood
New York 10546
USA

New Zealand

The New Zealand
  Alpine Garden
  Society
P.O. Box 2984
Christchurch
New Zealand

Further reading

Cartman, J. (1985) *Growing New Zealand Alpine Plants*, Reed Methuen, Auckland.

Elliott, R. C. (1969) *Alpines in Pots*, Alpine Garden Society, London.

Ellis, Entwhistle & Walkey (1993) *Pests and Diseases of Alpine Plants*, Alpine Garden Society, Pershore.

Grey-Wilson, C. (1988) *The Genus Dionysia*, Alpine Garden Society, Woking.

Harding, W. (1992) *Saxifrages*, Alpine Garden Society, Pershore.

Heath, R. E. (1981) *Collector's Alpines*, 2nd edition, Collingridge, London.

Horny, R., Webr, K. & Byam-Grounds, J. (1986) *Porophyllum Saxifrages*, Byam-Grounds, Stamford.

Lowe, D. B. (1991) *Growing Alpines in Raised Beds, Troughs and Tufa*, B. T. Batsford Ltd, London.

Polunin, A. & Stainton, A. (1984) *Flowers of the Himalaya*, Oxford University Press, Oxford.

Philipson, W. R. & Hearn, D. Rock *Garden Plants of the Southern Alps*, Caxton Press, Christchurch.

Rolfe, R. (1990) *The Alpine House*, Christopher Helm, Bromley / Timber Press, Portland, Oregon.

Smith, G. F. & Lowe, D. B. (1977) *Androsaces*, Alpine Garden Society, Woking.

Stainton, A. (1988) *Flowers of the Himalaya, A Supplement*, Oxford University Press, Oxford.

Webb, D. A. & Gornall, R. J. (1989) *Saxifrages of Europe*, Christopher Helm, Bromley / Timber Press, Portland, Oregon.

PLANT INDEX